Auburn Hills: A City is Born

To Otis Newkirk,

Congratulations to you for the positive role you continue to play in the development of your community.

Trent Pomeroy
11-13-08

Wilson L. Harmer
8-13-08

Auburn Hills: A City is Born

Trout Pomeroy

Copyright © 2008 by Trout Pomeroy.

Library of Congress Control Number: 2008902748
ISBN: Hardcover   978-1-4363-3128-9
                 Softcover   978-1-4363-3127-2

All rights reserved. No part of this book may be reproduced or transmitted in any form or by any means, electronic or mechanical, including photocopying, recording, or by any information storage and retrieval system, without permission in writing from the copyright owner.

This book was printed in the United States of America.

To order additional copies of this book, contact:
Xlibris Corporation
1-888-795-4274
www.Xlibris.com
Orders@Xlibris.com
40010

Contents

Part 1
A City Is Born..11

Part 2
A City Takes Identity...57

Part 3
A City Comes of Age...93

About the Writer..107

Special thanks to

Robert and Vivian Grusnick—Former Township Supervisor, Charter Commissioner, and first Mayor of the City of Auburn Hills, and his supportive wife
Leonard Hendricks—Former City Manager
Wilson Garner—Chairman, Auburn Hills Historical Society
Michael Davis—Charter Commissioner and City Council member
Dale Fisk—Chairman of the Charter Commission and City Council member
Ron Shirley—Former Township Trustee and member of the first City Council
Veronica New—Former City Clerk and member of Document Review Committee
Helen Venos—Former City Clerk and member of Document Review Committee
Frederick Cromie—Principal of Avondale High School
Bob Newman—Citizen
Michael Culpepper—City Manager, City of Auburn Hills
Jim Seeterlin—Former Supervisor of the Charter Township of Waterford and member of State Boundary Commission
Mayors Tom McMillin, Jim McDonald and Mari Edwards
Victoria Valko—City Treasurer
Stephanie Carroll and Bonita Pomeroy—Editors
Jeanetta Miller—Editor in Chief/Project Manager

Part 1

A City Is Born

A City Is Born

A city is born.

It is called Auburn Hills, and it has become a powerful force in the county north of Detroit, Michigan.

The City of Auburn Hills was incorporated in 1983, ushered in as a result of its populace mustering the moxie required to move forward, finessing a myriad of challenges, engaging prerogatives, prevailing in the voting booths of the community, and willfully opting for all the glory and potential headaches of being a city as opposed to being a township.

A majority of voters stepped up and said, "What the heck, let's try this."

Consciously, soberly, and with modest swagger, they set in motion a sequence of events that forever delivered this provincial semblance of civilization in the sticks of Oakland County into an exceedingly proud and full-blown expression of contemporary urbanity.

Twenty-five years have now passed since what was Pontiac Township took the ascent to cityhood, adapting Auburn Hills as the best expression anyone could come up with to identify an area, a place in time, a slivery upside-down L of seventeen square miles of civic entity.

History shows a township became a city. The anniversary of any such event cries out for reflection, and the vantage point of twenty-five years after the fact is as good as any place from which all involved can savor the aftermath of such a weighty occasion.

In this case, a uniquely proud township became an unusually brilliant city, and that only adds luster to what would already, ordinarily be a captivating chronology.

Incorporation in what became the City of Auburn Hills was a long time coming, and it will be a long time gone.

Achieving it was a mountainous accomplishment and a masterful work of political art—a stunning achievement no matter how you slice it.

Just what special chemistry sets the process in motion now hovers as the essential question surrounding this rather astounding civic development.

Two words—*faith* **and** *belief*—provide an explanation.

In the case of Auburn Hills becoming a city, faith and belief set the tone for eventual transition of historic proportion.

Without a doubt, the conviction of its citizenry turned the tide. Their perseverance set in motion sheer transformation.

Certainly, it was nothing short of amazing when what had been a decidedly low-key township in the sticks transitioned over several years, becoming a shining beacon of countrified urbanity.

Let the record state clearly: it was *the people* of Auburn Hills who affected municipal revolution by daring to envision their surroundings as worthy of incorporation.

Their faith was in themselves and in their own capacity to effect such an ambitious arrangement.

Belief was the other component.

Willingly, with their eyes wide open, the people of the area bought into the rhetoric of their government leaders, who assured them they could gain and manage incorporation.

They suspended disbelief and instead embraced belief, believing that progress relies on gumption, guts, and an inclination to roll the dice when the odds seem good.

Incorporation was sold to them as a product, and they decided to buy it—lock, stock, and bylaws.

Incorporation was presented as the only binding way to preserve the past, enhance the present, and earn the future.

The bold point of view was expressed so persistently and persuasively that the citizens came to believe in the optimism that was presented to them.

Faith and belief brought out the momentum required to certify the birth of an incredibly vibrant and vital "city in the hills"—the hills of what was always known as "Auburn," something or other—give or take half a dozen variants on the theme.

The story of how an unassuming township could possibly summon up and unleash the collective wherewithal required to pull off such a stunning achievement is flat out captivating.

Surely, this modern-day saga abounds in anecdotes, tales of valor, and civic heroism.

Auburn Hills: A City is Born

Auburn Hills, as we know it today, emerged from a thick shroud of unlikely circumstances.

That it did, in fact, eventually become a city in spite of many obstacles along the way is testament to the power of a committed cadre of citizens who stood tall in building the city of their dreams.

Real people made Auburn Hills a reality.

It was all as simple—and as wonderfully complex—as that.

The present-day City of Auburn Hills has a history colorful as its lush rolling terrain, a legacy rich as its cumulative wealth.

Characterized today by architectural magnificence, awe-inspiring corporate headquarters, immaculate residential neighborhoods, and persistent retail, educational, and entertainment activity, Auburn Hills was once an entirely noiseless haven, dripping in distinct pastoral tranquility.

In its prior iteration as the Township of Pontiac, the woodsy and remote community located between Pontiac and Rochester was an unpretentious mix of hope, harmony, and collective aspiration.

These elements and more convened in the early 1980s to help catapult once-sleepy Pontiac Township into the City of Auburn Hills—one of dynamic Oakland County's busiest and most vibrant municipalities.

The story of how a city was born is a tale replete in steely vision and applied political capability on the part of a sneaky-smart core of early civic leaders. Their persistence in accomplishing what once seemed entirely unlikely is revealed as a singular "perfect storm" of momentum-building grassroots civic accomplishment.

Even the term *once-sleepy* didn't exactly apply to this area in 1807 when the United States gained possession of its land.

The arrangement occurred under terms of a treaty with Indian tribes of the area, including Ottawa, Chippewa, Wyandot, and Potawatomi tribes. In fact, it was the great Ottawa Chief Pontiac, a leader of seminal significance whose name gave identity to a place.

With the arrival of European influence, the purity of Indian presence began to recede.

It gave way slowly to an increasingly diverse mix of French trappers, British militarists, devout Jesuits, eager explorers, and eventually to Anglo-American settlers, the first of whom came paddling upstream in canoes to the area along the Clinton River.

Soon others found their way north from Detroit into the hinterlands, inching out into the wilds along primal Indian trails, the most significant of which traced a route connecting Detroit and Saginaw, passing through what became the City of Pontiac. (That "trail" became Woodward Avenue, evoking a fine median strip and, much later, a Dream Cruise.)

In 1821, the first area settlement began in what is now the City of Auburn Hills. Known as the Village of Auburn, it opened its first school in 1824. Graduates of that bare-bones institution opened the small village's earliest stores and shops, setting in place the beginnings of what one day would become a complex and fully functional community with a multimillion-dollar annual budget.

The original design of Pontiac Township was a rolling composite of rivers, lakes, and land. In its earliest form, it was comprised of about thirty-six square miles of rambling real estate, factoring in a bog or two.

Much of that area eventually reverted to adjacent communities, primarily the City of Pontiac.

Early settlers had followed the original Indian population that inhabited the marshy area, showing up on the south side of the Clinton River in 1821.

A gristmill was completed in 1824, and the future of a modest settlement was thereby assured.

What happened here also occurred in other fledging centers of early organized existence throughout Oakland County; where there were rivers, there were also early stirrings of commerce fostered by the magnetic appeal of mills and the power they generated.

Rivers beget mills, which beget small manufacturing, ensuring civil interaction and residential and commercial development.

From general nothingness emerged General Motors.

Defining Identity

Established in 1827 as Michigan's third township by Governor Lewis Cass, Pontiac Township was then (and remains now) inhabited by innovative and industrious individuals and, soon, a rich mixture of institutions. A decidedly can-do spirit unified its early inhabitants and lent early identity to its emerging aura as perceived not only by their own selves, but also by the outside world.

The community became identified with oblique principles like honesty, accomplishment, and perseverance—at least to the extent any area could presumably embody the perception of such noble virtues.

The Auburn Heights/Pontiac Township area exuded a special flavor, internally and externally, in the centuries and decades proceeding incorporation.

Irregular in shape and lacking a distinct downtown center, it more than made up for those limitations by revealing itself as a uniquely self-confident community inhabited by a spunky aggregate of no-nonsense entrepreneurs and social activists.

Early on, emerging rivalries between what became the City of Auburn Hills and the City of Pontiac were apparent.

When Michigan became a territory in January 1805, then Governor William Hull negotiated peace treaties with the Indian tribes. His successor, Lewis Cass, set forth a proclamation in 1819 to establish boundaries within the emerging Oakland County.

Historian Lillian D. Avery noted the choice of location of the county seat was an early source of rivalry between the then Village of Auburn and the Village of Pontiac. She said the latter won out because Auburn did not have the financial backing that Pontiac did.

Others assert Auburn's population was growing faster than Pontiac's population, which tilted the county seat equation its way. But Pontiac had more power mill sites, and its main "intersection" at the time of the Clinton River and the old Saginaw Trail made it a more likely site.

In any event, early settlers founded Auburn in approximately 1821.

A Canadian, Elijah Thornton, "squatted on the south side of the Clinton River a little above where the Grand Trunk Western's Amy Station now stands," James Wilson wrote in the March 20, 1958, edition of the *Auburn Heights Sentinel.*

The first permanent settler, Wilson added, was Aaron Webster, who named this new community after the City of Auburn, New York. Webster favored Auburn for its affordability and commercial potential, and soon made arrangements to take over Thornton's holdings.

Quickly, he built a dam and millrace. He was then stricken with typhoid fever and died, giving way to Ebenezer Smith and son, who assumed his interests and eventually finished construction of a gristmill.

Captain Hervey Parke laid out the original Village of Auburn in 1826 and set up shop with fellow proprietors I. L. Smith, Sylvestor Smith, Elizur Goodrich, and Aaron Smith. In 1823, a post office was in place; in 1825, a school and a hotel.

"There was a village green surrounded by attractive homes," Wilson wrote. Add in a decent tavern, a Baptist church, blacksmith shops, and two general stores, and what you had was basically an extremely decent community in the making.

The banks of the Clinton were gently and beautifully elevated on either side. "The water privilege is rarely surpassed and exceeded by none in the territory," an excerpt from the *Oakland Chronicle* noted in 1830.

Fifty buildings and three hundred inhabitants gave definition to Auburn as it first gained a sense of self. Men of capital and enterprise came along engendering major momentum, setting the stage for bold new roads and other infrastructures.

Then things began to slow. Wilson said Auburn reached its zenith about this time and remained relevant only until about 1850. At which point it slipped back into more of a small country village type of setting, with an emphasis on *small.*

On the other hand, there has never been anything slight or disproportionately out of formula about the spunk of the people who have called Auburn home, from its humble origin to its slightly incredible present sense of vitality.

Its residents have shared in common an abiding sense of loyalty to one another and to the legacy of their small slice of heaven in the former Michigan Territory.

Their singular zeal gave identity to this area, distinguishing it as a tangible example of what happens when any small mass of moderately ambitious and capable people put down roots in a common area and set their collective minds on the shared goal of building a community worth living and working in.

Community Expands, Gains Definition

Dusty roads and colloquial settings eventually gave way to today's ultramodern identity as a highly confident kingdom unto itself populated by more than twenty thousand purposeful residents. Transformation came slowly, but certainly.

As the former village evolved, the strong foundation of community that coalesced over the years proved to be most hospitable to a grand, new city.

Evidence of this is on display throughout the present-day Auburn Hills, now home to several strong church congregations, literally hundreds of boldly innovative companies, concerns, and other organized expressions of commerce, entertainment, education, medicine, and research.

In 1983, when Pontiac Township finally slipped into its nicest wardrobe and stepped out into the world as the City of Auburn Hills, its past had become prologue in a decisive and dramatic way.

Those looking back on these events today will find it compelling to realize the culmination of incorporation occurred in 1983—twenty-five years in the rearview mirror of life through which we now perceive these events.

It was then area residents went to their election places. There in the quiet of tiny gymnasiums and small voting booths, those early citizens of the area did consciously reach a consensus.

With all their wits intact, they decided they did indeed firmly believe the proud niche of territory they inhabited as "one people" had the necessary ways and means to consider itself a city and to become one.

Today, of course, *it is* hard to imagine that doubt ever existed whether this township had what it would take to become a high-profile, fully legitimate city. Yet such skepticism did dominate common consensus. Doubt not only existed, it also defied many an imagination.

Looking around the present-day City of Auburn Hills—circa 2007/08—it's easy to discern the rationale for incorporation.

Overtly urban in many respects, the city is entirely logical unto itself. The place it became is a fully justified and complex municipal expression, complete with all the physical ingredients of any fully faceted and slightly brazen uptown setting.

But it wasn't always this way. And it's just warming up to what it will inevitably become—an advanced version of what it is still busy becoming.

Effort and Ardor

The City of Auburn Hills evolved from humble roots into a genuine citadel of high-energy activity, defining "quality of life" in nearly every conceivable measure of analysis.

This didn't happen automatically, of course. And therein lays the truth of any such discussion—something worth having doesn't come too easily. Ardor must accompany effort for any meaningful social progress to occur.

In the case of the City of Auburn Hills, ardor and effort cooked up a divine feast that fed the entire notion of incorporation to the point it satiated the wildest aspirations of an entire community.

The ultimate inception of Auburn Hills as a modern-day megacity was nothing more—or less—than a complete result of the organizational wherewithal of civic-minded area residents.

Their vision of an exemplary community lifted them over all barriers in their successful effort to achieve incorporation.

It didn't happen overnight.

But the promise of what they accomplished will light the sky over all the ages.

Once basically anonymous, it is now known around the world as a beacon of enterprise, education, and high technology.

Once an inconsequential "blip" on the map of northeastern Oakland County, the city that became Auburn Hills came to dominate the commercial and entertainment agenda of the entire Detroit metropolitan area.

Auburn Hills became "a huge deal."

Shaped Like an L

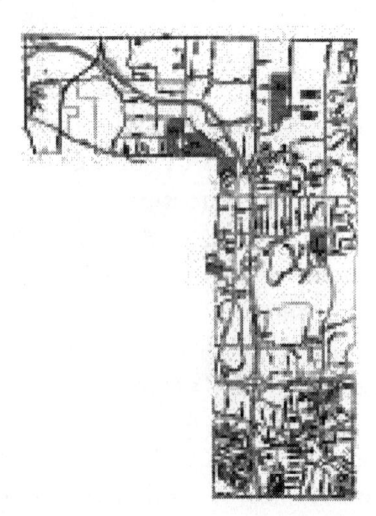

Shaped like an upside-down L, semirural as well, Pontiac Township in the late American twentieth century was a source of little consequence to some, a treasure to others.

As the Township of Pontiac, the general perception of its identity was obscured by the implicit stepchild-type relationship it maintained with its awesome neighbor to the west, the Mother City Pontiac, the industrial powerhouse of an abutting minimetropolis that offered its next-door township a small vestige of geographic recognition.

Only from within its seventeen-square-mile oddly configured circumference did Pontiac Township's faithful inhabitants know better.

Those unaware of Pontiac Township's special allure and quiet potential saw only fields, farms, and hilly roads—essentially uncivilized nature.

Those who lived there and experienced its comforts and delights knew better.

To the outside world, Pontiac Township was an incidental appendage on an adjacent industrial and residential center.

To its residents, however, this stretch of God's creation was blessed home almighty, a highly distinguishable and treasured community on the rise.

Surely, Chief Pontiac would be surprised by what happened to these holy acres in what was for eons considered to be largely untamed countryside. Or imagine how the good old Michigan boys who used to hang out at the Texaco station on Opdyke Road in the '50s might suck in their guts today if they could see the rush-hour traffic weaving into the Oakland Technology Park.

The present-day City of Auburn Hills emerged from an extremely proud traditional community of service-oriented citizens.

The story of the birth of what became a dynamic and highly visible city in the center of Oakland County is adorned with historic twists, setbacks that became learning experiences, and countless portrayals of large-scale personal valor.

It is a testament to what a small group of like-minded individuals can accomplish through their own shared vision and efforts with the consent of a citizenry whose trust was earned over time in the crucible of conflict and growth.

Early Efforts Stumble

The notion of incorporation in the land north and east of the City of Pontiac did not always enjoy widespread community support.

Even key state agencies whose mission it was to evaluate such possibilities were less than fully disposed to the idea, and there never appeared to be much of a shortage of categorical detractors to the concept of incorporation.

Those ranks were filled with individuals, who, for various reasons, saw such a development as a formula for failure.

Many were comfortable with the status quo for it represented keeping things as they had always been.

They favored the "no risk, no reward" paradigm. And their conservative instincts to not rock the boat nearly characterized the majority of the electorate in the former Pontiac Township.

The township could have just as easily remained as the same old township, but for a band of true believers who saw the long-term potential of some form of incorporation, they kept building the momentum to ensure its eventuality.

Fear, anxiety, and suspicion of the uncertainties of change stifled the aspirations of many residents.

Many expressed concerns that area taxpayers would be slaughtered by ever-spiraling layers of financial obligation.

Others felt existing services would prove to be inadequate and could collapse under the weight of the larger burdens associated with the traditional city form of government.

Efforts to research the legacy of incorporation in this community led to the discovery of handwritten minutes of Pontiac Township Board meetings dating back as far as 1942 when the issue surfaced in the public agenda.

On March 30 of that year, a "Special Meeting" was held at "the Clerk's home"—she being Anna M. Oakley.

Discussion centered on issues of creating special assessment rolls for financing fire protection programs in the township.

Soon, dedicated citizens established two fire districts in the old township. No longer did residents have to rely on the nearby City of Pontiac for firefighting assistance.

And the notion of autonomy in "the Heights" had become like the proverbial genie released from the bottle to the extent that a bold new future as an independent municipality became much easier to imagine and become self-fulfilling prophecy.

This specific topic on this specific date in now-ancient 1942 at Anna Oakley's home bears no binding relevance to the topic at hand.

Yet it is worth pointing out how a long and carefully thought-out process proceeded what eventually became serious talk of incorporation.

Formal organization of township civic affairs evolved meticulously over many decades of applied effort to assemble and operate an equitable arrangement of residential and commercial activity.

Early generations of citizens and township leaders had considerable "skin in the game" of building an increasingly functional and independent community.

Their commitment and considerable shared-sweat equity formed more than water and sewer systems, quality roads, and schools and civic institutions. It also helped congeal a coherent and mutually dependent core of people, all of whom chose to live here, work here, and put their entire existence on the line in a place within which they shared a deep and binding sense of shared affection.

Outsiders might have confused their well-earned sense of oneness as quaint or lacking in passion; those whose efforts produced the emerging core of a defined and forever-defining community knew better.

Call it Amy, call it Auburn Heights, call it whatever you want—something profound and eternally certain had, over a long period, seeped into and within the lives of those who called this place home.

When the notion of incorporation first started kicking up its heels around the homes and small businesses of the area in the late twentieth century, those inculcations assured the idea would have legs, considerable legs indeed.

But like all things worthwhile, incorporation did not happen overnight.

Unlikely Indeed

That a township could become a city was as improbable as ping-pong in a cyclone. There were too many dominant inhibitors.

For one thing, there weren't enough people here, and those people who were here had about as much interest in incorporation as they did in the behavior of immature larvae.

Lacking in pomposity, the early citizenry of the Auburn Heights area defined cultural humility; they went about their lives with a virtual absence of arrogance or anything resembling progressive. They were classic "simple folk," innately normal down-home people who sat around swatting flies on their front porches, grew zucchinis, and kept farm animals long after most residents of nearby Bloomfield Township had taken up golf. They wore jeans, said "shoot," and put the *M* in *modest*. They were self-proclaimed "white socks" people who felt pride in their affinity for country behaviors such as being nice to one another and racing motorcycles up earthen mountains late into the night and into the wee hours of the morning. They liked attending the local small churches of the time together and enjoyed spending their spare hours doing things like erecting birdbaths alongside an occasional abandoned cement mixer.

Pontiac Township almost forever was a throwback to an era past, a place where people could forget about trying to impress one another with the cars in their driveways or the size of their exterior decking. Residents kept barnyard animals and didn't care what city folk thought about them as long as they didn't throw their pop cans on the dirt roads that lined this peculiarly shaped island in modernity.

Incorporation for virtual eons was something like a joke, a bad joke at that.

Look at it this way: if it—let's call it Auburn—wanted to become a city, it would have done it long before it actually did indeed do so.

The community was instinctively reluctant to pull the trigger on incorporation. Why? Because their trigger fingers never itched enough for all of them to want to go to all the trouble related to such a far-reaching and legally complicated enterprise.

Amy or Auburn Heights or whatever they were calling it at the time had no real fire in the belly for anything resembling organized civic coalescing. The people of the area were more about the task of daily living as defined by middle-class mores of the time—also known as bowling, baking, and being true to their own nature.

The community was quietly content. For most of antiquity, it only wanted to be left alone to get a good night's sleep.

Nevertheless, by around 1960 or 1970 or so, the giant was awakened so to speak. Natural developments, within and without, rang the alarm.

And so it transpired that "the hicks" became city slickers after all and lived to tell about it, with smiles on their faces and pride in their hearts.

As recently as 1970, the then township supervisor led a petition drive to incorporate the Township of Pontiac into the City of Pontiac Heights.

In spite of much initial enthusiasm, the effort failed quite miserably.

The number of signatures needed was 5 percent of the population—14,668 at the time.

Nine optimistic citizens of the township took it upon themselves to circulate petitions, including

- Irene Bates
- Carl A. Schingeck
- William Kent

- Helen P. Kaye
- Charles A. Chandler Jr.
- Goldie B. Mailahn
- Robert W. Grusnick
- John C. Richardson
- Roy Wahl

At first, it seemed the group's commitment to change would yield desirable results.

A public hearing was conducted in September 1970 to determine whether the township would be allowed to place an incorporation proposal on the ballot.

According to James S. Hyde, executive secretary of the State Boundary Commission, the purpose of the hearing was to enable residents of the Pontiac area to "contribute information on the proposed City of Pontiac Heights."

With this input, the commission had three choices:

1. Decide to deny the incorporation petitions.
2. Elect to totally approve them.
3. Approve them with adjustments in proposed boundaries.

Petitions for incorporation containing the signatures of 282 residents were filed with the commission in March 1969 by then Township Supervisor Roy Wahl.

Wahl said at the time, "We had to do it. We have lived in fear of annexation (by Pontiac) in the township for several years."

Township officials noted that the basis for that fear had been the annexation of 265 acres of land by the city since 1965.

In 1970 the township had seventeen square miles of land, excluding roads, with a population of nearly fourteen thousand. Land value of the township was estimated at $46 million.

Poor Cousins Personified

An editorial published in the *Pontiac Press* on September 14, 1970, said "a good case" had been made by the petitioners.

With its population booming, incorporation as a city would give the to-be-chosen government the power to levy mills on property to meet the needs of the quickly emerging municipality—up to twenty mills depending on charter provisions.

However, other issues cooled the rapture of editorial writers who opined against the action. Their arguments captured the essence of objection.

"We feel incorporation of the Township into a new city will not properly meet the needs of the residents there, nor of the area," they wrote. "There is no real need for a separate government, fractionalizing and duplicating services.

"If and when the area is incorporated it should join the City of Pontiac. This will provide Township residents with a full range of services at a lower cost."

In 1970, the newspaper noted, the City of Pontiac had over half a billion dollars in valuation.

"The outlook (for Pontiac) is extremely bright for expansion of the present industrial complex and construction of the $125-million Pontiac Plan for downtown," they wrote. "The proposed new city would be a poor cousin at best."

In summary, the local daily newspaper pooh-poohed the idea of incorporation for the township.

"We feel that creation of a new city from the odd-shaped land involved would saddle the residents with high costs but not be able to service them adequately, and that the proposal violates sound long-range planning principles."

After the petitions were filed with the Michigan Boundary Commission, the township board requested and was granted a meeting with Joe A. Parisi, then the executive director of the Michigan Township Association. Parisi toured the township and observed the facilities before the meeting.

He made a verbal presentation to the board, and a question-and-answer session followed.

Then, to the surprise of many, the board authorized the director to request that the boundary commission stop the process.

Parisi didn't feel the township was ready for incorporation. He said in order to maintain economic stability, the area should be 55 percent industrial and commercial.

To reach this balance, the director inferred rather directly that the community needed to update both its facilities and overall infrastructure. Other smaller issues entered the equation, but none of them bore as directly on this outcome as the overall preparation issue.

The petitioners and others with dreams of incorporation had work to do as a community in order to ever again entertain such thoughts of municipal grandeur.

The State Boundary Commission took the following actions:

> *Pursuant to the order of the State Boundary Commission, we return herewith the petition in the entitled matter as is required by the second sentence of section 8 of Act 191 of the Public Acts of 1968, being 123.1208 of the Compiled Laws of 1948, and certify that attached hereto is a true copy of the Commission's order stating its reasons for rejecting said petition.*

And so it was back to the drawing board for those future-minded residents of increasingly less obscure Pontiac Township to chart a course for achieving city status and try to marshal meaningful consensus for incorporation within the community.

As difficult as it must have been for those hoping to help guide the community toward incorporation, this apparent setback turned out to be more of a learning experience. They were down, but not out.

Parisi took township officials to school. In announcing the outcome of Round One, he also simultaneously ensured the arrival of Round Two in which the struggle for incorporation would turn the way of the "getting smarter" petitioners.

During the 1970s, a change had been affected in the Charter Township Act that gave protection of boundaries to communities.

This document was filed with the state on September 2, 1978. In addition, the Charter Township Act defined the responsibilities of township officials and gave more direct responsibilities to the supervisor, who in this case at this juncture was Robert W. Grusnick. Among other things, the rate of mills was set, a figure not to exceed five mills. The fiscal year was changed according to the charter to follow the calendar year January 1 through December 31, as opposed to the previous fiscal year of April 1 through March 31.

The significance of these apparently minor revisions would be borne out in the years to come.

Awesome Developments in Area Hasten Incorporation

Monumental events of eternal significance erupted near and around the former Township of Pontiac in the years that passed immediately before the eventual vote to become the City of Auburn Hills.

Viewed in tandem, they reveal the extent to which larger external activities helped foster an environment in which the logic of incorporation settled in the thought processes of township residents.

Here is a partial summary of some of the galactic changes that occurred "way back" in township days, within and around the periphery of what became—rather miraculously—the current city.

- In 1975, the stage was set for more ambitious civic structuring to occur when the township purchased a portion of what was known as the old Wesson-Seyburn Estate at 1827 N. Squirrel Road. That the original township was established in 1827 wasn't irony lost on community activists at the time. In fact, the mingling of parallel address and founding date numbers was like a cosmic spark that galvanized their dream and visited a certain sense of manifest destiny in their minds. In the next year, the old township established its present-day Civic Center on and around the vast property. The 37.5-acre amalgam of vintage buildings is comprised of more than one dozen city offices and structures, including an enchanting, state-of-the-art library, as well as police, fire, and all other primary municipal offices. This transcendent accomplishment did wonders to boost civic pride and reveal the physical potential of incorporation as embodied in a beautiful and impressive array of reconditioned buildings that formed a most charming campus configuration. Certainly, this acquisition and major enhancement of these properties paved the way for greater gestures of unity among citizens and business/corporate concerns. With such an impressive "home," becoming a city in many ways emerged as the next logical step toward sublime respectability.

- Beginning in 1970, construction that would forever change the hue of this area of Oakland County and Pontiac Township commenced upon what became known as the Pontiac Silverdome. It was, and remains, a massive structure constructed on a sprawling plot of land located immediately west of Pontiac Township at the southwest corner of Opdyke and Featherstone roads. Officially opened in 1975, the Silverdome (also known as the Pontiac Metropolitan Stadium or PonMet Stadium) quickly became a major new center of gravity in the metropolitan Detroit area. Physically awesome, its presence was symbolically even larger. The domed stadium was built at a cost of $55.7 million and featured an original silver roof built of Teflon-coated fiberglass panels that were supported by air pressure inside the stadium. Almost instantly, the domed stadium was a center of intense activity. It was home of the Detroit Lions; the Detroit Pistons; the now-defunct Michigan Panthers from the USFL; annual Michigan state high school football playoffs; world-class wrestling matches; World Cup soccer; truck pulls, trade shows, special events; the 1979 NBA All-Star game; concerts featuring mega-performers such as U2, Pink Floyd, Elvis Presley, the Rolling Stones, The Who, and Led Zeppelin; and the never-to-be-forgotten 1987 appearance of Pope John Paul II, whose presence in the vicinity cast such solemnity on the entire area some believe it hovers still. Even Super Bowl XVI was played on its synthetic field on one of the coldest days in state history, January 24, 1982. The only event that rivaled that legendary game, pitting the Cincinnati Bengals against the San Francisco 49ers, or the Pope's appearance, was WrestleMania III on March 29, 1987, when 93,173 fans attended a fervently stupendous event to see Hulk Hogan battle Andre the Giant. Having the Silverdome as a next-door neighbor—living so close to you the smell of its exhaust plumes was palpable—unquestionably did more to change the dynamics of potential incorporation in the previously low-keyed township than did any other historic development. Its massive presence cast the entire area into a state of imminent redefinition. The sheer magnitude of the Silverdome standing there glistening in the sun like some gigantic luminescent rock fallen from the sky staggered the mind and in a very strong sense precipitated the inevitability of change to come. Opdyke Road, over time, became a high-growth corridor with new offices and businesses happily burgeoning along its path. M-59, another busy expressway that extends through the area in an east-west direction, also saw new business complexes springing up along its increasingly busy asphalt surface. The establishment of the Silverdome in what the late Detroit Mayor Coleman Young referred to as "the cornfields of Oakland County" had a radical impact on the entire region and particularly on Pontiac Township. Big-time sporting events and other high-profile happenings brought the Detroit area and soon the rest of the world to the immediate doorstep of what had been, only a few years before, indistinct, relatively unknown, and underappreciated quasi-boondocks. With Billy Sims lighting it up on the field and crowds exceeding eighty thousand people showing up on an increasingly frequent basis, a large portion of the real world had been dropped onto the eastern edge of Pontiac, which had the predictable effect on its township/neighbor of inducing a rather rare variant of community mania. The mighty dome casting light atop this sprawling structure signaled a new day had arrived in the ravines of this idyllic paradise.

- In 1980, the General Motors Corporation announced that another king-sized parcel at the southern end of Orion Township would become the home of a new, multimillion-dollar assembly plant. It would be built on acreage west of Lapeer Road, between Silver Bell and Brown roads, the latter happening to abut Pontiac Township. Almost immediately, the inevitable followed. By 1981, developers had begun scrambling to acquire and improve industrially zoned land and acquire permits to use that land in Pontiac Township, in the area near the new GM facility. Soon legal actions were engaged involving what became the City of the Village of Lake Angelus, the Township of Orion, among others, regarding the dispensation and codification of property adjacent to the new action and additional legal issues. As GM built its Orion assembly plant, every community within shooting distance responded with unmistakably vigorous interest, sharing among each other an intelligent awareness that a project of this magnitude had the capacity to change everything in its wake, quickly, permanently, and for better or worse. For Pontiac Township, a new industrial facility on its northern edge equated to opportunity knocking with sledgehammer force.

- As early as 1974, immediately to its east, the former Avon Township had also begun looking at becoming a city. Seven years later, township officials again sought hearings with the Michigan State Boundary Commission for the purpose of reassessing questions regarding the validity of past petition signatures. Affidavits appeared, and arguments were aired out. In time, clarification was visited on the process, leading the commission in June 1981 to reverse an earlier decision, confirming the validity of signatures. At the time, the thirty-five-square-mile township had a population of forty-two thousand. Responding to an attempt from the adjacent City of Rochester to annex a 2.2-square-mile portion of land, township officials chose to fight annexation until a long legal process apparently ended with state and federal judges concluding Rochester could have the land. By 1982, a charter commission was elected ushering in the eventual adaptation of incorporation for what in 1983 became the City of Rochester Hills.

- To the south, the expansion of suburbia surged with certainty toward the boundaries of Pontiac Township. Troy experienced phenomenal residential and commercial development as did Bloomfield Township and other surrounding areas, evoking considerable "shock and awe" in the old Pontiac Township. Newcomers were breathing at the gates of former boundaries becoming mere geographic distinctions, and abutting communities were imploding upon one another. In the hinterland that became the City of Auburn Hills, the reverberations of suburban encroachment were forebodingly clear. Those who were aware of such trends and happened to feel a sense of responsibility to maintain the integrity and identity of their homes and community responded to these developments with a hastened sense of urgency. A monstrous explosion of people and enterprise had sounded throughout central Oakland County, leaving investors, entrepreneurs, *and* municipalities to scramble for a new place at a larger table.

Pontiac Forces the Issue

The story of the eventual chartering of the City of Auburn Hills continued most logically in the nearby City of Pontiac.

On December 14, 1976, at a meeting of the city council, Resolution No. 403 to annex 6.6 acres from the Township of Pontiac was made and passed.

The area, at the southwest corner of Featherstone and Opdyke roads, was (and still is) used by the Silverdome Stadium.

To say this action in nearby Pontiac caught the attention of the residents of Pontiac Township would be a great understatement.

If there was anything that the apparent majority of residents wanted, it was to stay detached from the civic auspices of its urban neighbor. Resistance to annexation became the deciding incentive to incorporation as an independent city.

In January 1977, Pontiac Township claimed that Pontiac was "gerrymandering" city boundaries to annex a potentially tax-rich undeveloped parcel of land in the township just east of the Silverdome Stadium.

Township officials cited their fears of possible "extinction" on January 5, 1977, when they asked Oakland Circuit Court to void Pontiac's December 14, 1976, annexation of a small chunk of land located in the Silverdome parking lot.

The township said the move served no benefit to Pontiac residents but would permit the city to leapfrog its boundary along Opdyke Road for future annexation of 120 acres of prime development land in the township.

At the time, active proposals were in play for what was then regarded to be a possible $20 million hockey-basketball arena plus bars, restaurants, office and apartment buildings, and a luxury hotel for the 120-acre site.

Bob Grusnick, then as township supervisor, said in recent years that the township had spent about $12 million to provide water and sewer facilities to the surrounding area in anticipation of the development.

In the suit, township officials said that if Pontiac's annexation of the parking lot parcel was upheld, the city could try to annex the 120-acre site.

Grusnick said Pontiac officials had also approached owners of undeveloped land in the northern part of the township about cooperating with annexation bids by the city. Pontiac legal officials said at the time they felt the annexation was legal.

On January 5, Circuit Judge Alice F. Gilbert issued a temporary restraining order voiding the transaction until city officials could appear for a hearing on the matter.

The December 14 annexation involved a triangular nine-acre parcel on the southwest corner of Opdyke and Featherstone roads. The land in question was about five hundred feet wide and one thousand eight hundred feet long.

If upheld, it would have made city property contiguous along the entire western edge of the 120-acre site. That site is bounded by Opdyke, Featherstone, I-75, and M-59.

The township contended that state law required the city to own the land and that it would be a park or vacant for annexation without a hearing before the State Boundary Commission. Neither condition had been met.

City officials asserted at the time their only objective was to bring all of the stadium property inside city limits.

The Bob and Dorothy Show

In 1977 before the dust had settled on the issue, Township Supervisor Bob Grusnick and Treasurer Dorothy Babb traveled to the State Capitol in Lansing to discuss incorporation with the Michigan township executive and eventually with the Michigan Boundaries Commission.

The township director suggested that the local officials do two things

- Circulate incorporation petitions
- Then, presumably after the petitions had been certified by the state, oppose the incorporation of the City of Meadowbrook

In their own minds, the supervisor and treasurer believed that in pursuing the second rather curious objective they would in effect delay annexation-related actions for at least two years. But that meant they would have to face the issue again—not a good choice in their opinion.

As they visited with the Boundaries Commission executive secretary, further details emerged in the discussion. A "Timeline for Incorporation" emerged, delineating approval sequences from preparation activities to circulation, filing, and adjudication. Incorporation petitions were requested and rendered. Within this document the following important caveat was expressed in bold format:

> *If the incorporation is approved by referendum, then a charter must be adopted within two years of the date the approval order becomes effective.*

It went on to add that if a charter was not adopted within two years, the incorporation process would end.

General strategies were identified, and the two visitors from Oakland County left the meeting, feeling confident they understood the terms of the mission they sought to undertake.

Driving home that day, they encountered a snowstorm of historic proportions itself. Road navigation became very treacherous, an ominous sign implying some presence of similar threats to their civic-minded dreams.

According to local lore, one of the parties spent most of the trip stretched out on the backseat of the car. So perilous were the snowy roads and fields along the way. Despite the odds, the supervisor and the treasurer made it home safely that day. And the vision of a new city was soon to be realized.

Back among their colleagues and friends, the elected township officials met informally with the board. The august body wanted to proceed with filing an injunction through the Oakland County Circuit Court that would stop the City of Pontiac action until a hearing was held.

In the meantime, the board also wanted the petitions brought up to date with proper legal description and wording.

Petitions were ready to circulate in early February 1977.

Two sets of petitions were circulated.

One did not include the 6.6 acres in question that were in the circuit court for disposition; the other petition included the acreage in question.

The petitions were circulated at the same time and day.

Those days were

- Friday, February 4—after 5:00 PM
- Saturday, February 5
- Sunday, February 6

Compounding the difficulty in rallying support among the township citizenry was the buildup of nearly one foot of fresh snow on the ground and temperatures that hovered in the single-digit range.

In this effort, a total of forty-three citizens were circulators.

The following citizens were circulators:

- Lester Axford
- Valerie Bates
- Theodore G. Burkland
- Thrulin E. Cloud
- Larry G. Douglas
- Ruth J. Fisk
- Dorothy M. Gauthier
- Robert C. Hester
- David L. Jerrell
- Daun A. Mercer
- Dora M. Perry
- Ronald R. Shirley
- Walter G. Smith
- Cynthia L. Thompson
- Gary E. White
- Dorothy Babb
- Helen M. Boone
- Dennis O. Burtch
- Charles Dean
- Archibald Farrell
- Larry E. Flanigan
- Robert W. Grusnick
- Joseph L. Hopper
- Steve E. Lehozky

- Harry J. Mero
- Robert F. Rayner
- Ernest Simas Jr.
- Robert H. Hood
- Mildred A. Thorpe
- Devan Bates Jr.
- Eleanor Buero
- Ronald Burtch
- William F. Devereaux
- E. Dale Fisk
- Bernard P. Gauthier
- John A. Hamilton
- Richard T. Hupp
- Gerald G. Lonnstrom
- Veronica C. New
- Sharon L. Rayner
- Robert Smith
- Leo O. Strohschein
- Glenn E. Weiler

Again the number of valid signatures needed was 5 percent of the population of 14,668—which worked out to be 734 signatures.

There were over 1,200 signatures on both petitions submitted by The Group of 43.

Many at the time considered that number something of a minor miracle, given the inclement weather conditions and the additional challenge of completing two petitions at the same time.

Momentum was clearly evident.

A petition asking for the incorporation of most of Pontiac Township into the City of Meadowbrook was filed February 7, 1977.

An interoffice memo circulated within the State of Michigan Department of Treasury regarding Pontiac Township incorporation detailed efforts to verify signatures submitted.

In May 1977, staff members concluded the petitions contained an adequate number of valid signatures to render petitions of Docket No. 77-I-1 valid and sufficient. The following procedure was to be adhered to consistent with timelines established by the State Boundaries Commission.

On May 3 and May 9, 1977, the *Oakland Press* published the following "Notice of Right to Referendum on Becoming a Charter Township":

> *Official Information has been received from the Secretary of State of the State of Michigan, indicating that the township of Pontiac, has attained a population of 5,000 or more. This being the case, the township board has the right to exercise one of three options concerning township status as a charter township under the provisions of Act 90 of 1976.*
>
> *(1) Adopt, by majority vote, a resolution opposed to incorporation.*

(2) Adopt, by majority vote, a resolution of intent to approve incorporation.

(3) Adopt, by majority vote, a resolution to place before the electorate the question of incorporation at the next regular or special township election.

In the event option (2) is adopted by the township board, the citizens of the township have the option to file a 'Right to Referendum Petition.' This petition must be filed within the 60 days which must lapse between the passage of a resolution of intent to incorporate and the final passage of the resolution to incorporate as a charter township.

The petition will follow, in general terms, the nominating petition form as prescribed in the Michigan Election Law, Section 168.544© and in the heading will indicate "disagreement of intent to incorporate as a charter township." The petition must be signed by not less than 10% of the registered voters of the township based on the vote cast for all candidates for supervisor at the last election at which a supervisor was elected.

If the petition is successful, the question of incorporation will be placed on the ballot at the next general township or special township election.

The notice was attributed to Veronica New, Pontiac Township clerk.

Donald Oakes Enters Fray

The township retained the services of Government Affairs Consultant Donald Oakes to help guide the process and maintain adherence to prescribed timelines. Oakes emerged as a key figure in streamlining the campaign to become a city.

Soon, meaningful results began to surface.

On July 20, 1977, Village of Lake Angelus President Robert C. Lake wrote to the State Boundary Commission criteria analyst regarding the commission's invitation to the village to comment on the pending petition for incorporation of a portion of Pontiac Township as the City of Meadowbrook.

Noting the village lies partially within the territorial limits of Pontiac Township and partially within the territorial limits of Waterford Township, he pointed out village property owners pay taxes to the respective townships and receive governmental services, including police and fire protection, from them.

To summarize a complex set of considerations, Lake surmised the proposed incorporation would result in the withdrawal of existing governmental services from township areas lying outside of the proposed city boundary.

For this reason, he noted, the proposed incorporation would appear to affect the vital interests of the Village of Lake Angelus.

With this in mind, Lake told the commission the village wished to preserve its governmental autonomy.

He cited additional concerns relative to organizational questions and cited other pending questions and unresolved points of clarification.

"The Village of Lake Angelus does not oppose the proposed incorporation (of the then Township) but believes that the foregoing problems and concerns should be clarified and resolved as a condition of the incorporation."

Writing at the same time to the Pontiac Township Board, Lake said a major concern of the village was the withdrawal of existing police and fire protection services from that part of the village which lies within Pontiac Township.

Village officials had been informally advised that such services would be made available to the village under contract with the newly incorporated city.

Lake suggested such advisements be made formal as a matter of public record in the form of a resolution adopted by the Pontiac Township Board.

Incorporation Resolution

At its regular board meeting on July 25, 1977, Township Trustee Dale Fisk moved that it be resolved that members of the Board of Pontiac Township "do hereby give their support to the proposition that the citizens of the Township of Pontiac be given the opportunity to determine their future as either a Township or as a City, according to a majority vote."

No trustees opposed the motion.

In making the motion, Fisk cited several contributing factors.

- The year 1977 celebrated the 150th anniversary of the establishment of the Township of Pontiac.
- The township had grown through the years into "a solid community, proud of its history and heritage."
- Through the intervening years, the township had been subjected to assaults on its boundaries through attempts at annexation.

A petition had been filed with the State Boundary Commission to consider incorporation of said township.

Later in 1977, petitions were submitted to the State Boundary Commission, which would subsequently grant the status of incorporation to Pontiac Township that had sought to ward off further annexation attempts by neighboring cities.

To restate a key point, the move to incorporate Pontiac Township into a new city called Meadowbrook—as a means of protecting the township's interests in the Pontiac Silverdome area—was launched February 7, 1977, when Supervisor Grusnick submitted petitions bearing more than 1,200 names to the State Boundary Commission in Lansing.

Repeating another key fact, the action came as plans for a new multimillion-dollar sports arena and hotel development complex across from the Silverdome were being finalized.

A ruling on the legality of Pontiac's unilateral annexation of the parcel in December 1976 was pending before Oakland County Circuit Judge Alice Gilbert.

Grusnick told the *Oakland Press* he was confident the petitions would meet the boundary commission's requirements.

"We have a good cross section of the community from all ends of the township," he said. The request for incorporation would block any new annexation moves until residents were able to decide the incorporation question or an election was denied.

"The residents of Pontiac Township should be able to vote on their destiny without the threat of annexation," he said. "This move should afford the residents the opportunity to study the pros and cons and decide whether to become a city or remain a township."

Incorporation was perceived by Grusnick and others as the only way to protect the integrity of the township and its investment in water and sewer service to the area of the proposed sports arena.

"The way the law is now, there is no way that a general law township can protect its boundaries from annexation from a city," Grusnick said.

"The Township has gone on the hook to provide utilities for the Opdyke and Featherstone area. In my mind the tax base that is being created within the boundaries of Pontiac Township should stay within the township or the new city."

According to Grusnick, taxes were a concern of many residents, who asked whether living in the City of Meadowbrook would cost them more than living in Pontiac Township. Grusnick responded by saying any new tax rate would be indeterminate until a charter was presented to voters. Citizens were informed that under state law, cities are required to provide services such as road maintenance that townships are not required to provide. On the other hand, cities receive more revenue from state gasoline taxes than townships do.

The area included in the proposed City of Meadowbrook did not include the Village of Lake Angelus or a fifty-one-acre parcel south of Lake Angelus and not contiguous with the rest of the township.

In September 1977, the State Boundary Commission held a public hearing on the issue of incorporation for Pontiac Township. Citizens were given a chance to inform Lansing officials whether or not they supported the idea.

To influence those attending the hearing, township officials arranged to assemble the community's most impressive physical assets, including every major piece of firefighting equipment, in proximity to the meeting place. This effort to draw attention to the impressive scope of its largest pieces of municipal hardware was perceived at the time as "a dog and pony" show that could possibly bring bearing to emerging perceptions.

Prior to the hearing, Grusnick framed the question in frank terms.

"The issue," he said, "is whether the citizens want to unify and have an identity or face annexation to Pontiac. I think the people of the area have a right to protect their boundaries."

At the time, Grusnick said he saw no need for taxes to increase if incorporation was adopted. Any new services required would be more than offset by a new infusion of state gasoline tax revenue for road maintenance, he predicted, including prior statements regarding the existing capabilities of existing sewer and water systems.

On September 27, 1978, the following documents were filed at the Oakland County Clerk's Office and at the Secretary of State's Office in Lansing:

- Resolution of Intent to Approve Incorporation as a Charter Township
- Affidavit of Publication of Notice
- Certificate that no petition was filed requesting a referendum
- Certified copy of Resolution Incorporating as a Charter Township

Pontiac Seeks to Inhibit Township Incorporation Consensus

In October 1977, the City of Pontiac released a study that inferred Pontiac Township residents could face a tax increase of almost 40 percent if they approved incorporation as a city. Simultaneous to this, a consultant for the township said the claim was "for the birds." The study was prepared by the city's finance department. It was submitted to the State Boundary Commission in an effort to persuade the panel to deny the township's incorporation petition.

For his part, Oakes told the township board he felt the study made "some preposterous assumptions." Urging the board to file a strong rebuttal, he even alluded to the possibility the city had actually used false information.

"If you do not answer now, you lose your momentum and give credence to their allegations," Oakes implored the board. "I don't think you can be nice anymore about it. I think you have to answer fire with fire."

Subsequently, the board met in closed session with Oakes to plan a reaction to the ten-page study.

The document under consideration compared taxes and municipal costs for the two governmental entities. It implied the total tax rate for the new city's residents would rise from its current $52.36 per $1,000.00 of assessed property value to $72.91.

That figure included city, school district, Oakland Community College, intermediate school, county, and county drain taxes.

Study conclusions were based on a 1980 population of 22,000 for the new city—an increase of 7,000 over the then current estimated population.

Study predictions were dire indeed. Among other ominous projections it claimed

- The new city's residents would pay at least five mills in total taxes more than the City of Pontiac's residents for 1980.
- Spending for police services would more than quadruple in the new city and thirty-five new employees would have to be added.
- The cost of fire services per citizen would nearly triple.
- Government administrative costs would rise from the township's 1977 budget of $317,486 to over $1.1 million.

According to newspaper accounts at the time, Pontiac gave the report to the Boundary Commission on the last possible day it could do so. Interested parties had one month following a September public hearing on the incorporation petition for submission of testimony.

It was also submitted one day after owners of some of the township's most valuable property asked the Boundary Commission to exclude four hundred acres of land near the Silverdome from the incorporation petition. Reports indicated at least thirteen property owners wanted that land annexed to the City of Pontiac instead.

Grusnick maintained all along that the township already provided many of the services required of cities, and that taxes did not necessarily have to rise if the community incorporated.

Following release of the study, township officials busied themselves in chipping away at bits and pieces of the controversial documents while Pontiac officials said their numbers had been conservative, if anything, and that they could also participate in the exercise of second guessing projections.

A twelve-page rebuttal was released by the township through Grusnick's office that asked the Boundary Commission to "totally disregard" the figures used in Pontiac's study. "The information contained (in the cost study) is based on a series of assumptions and is fictitious," Grusnick said.

In a separate portion of the rebuttal, township officials said they expected township population in four years to be about 17,155—not the twenty-two thousand mentioned in the study.

Township and city officials sparred over fire department expenses. City officials argued the township—if it became a city—would have to replace its volunteer fire department with a forty-eight-person full-time force.

Township leaders like Grusnick countered that the nearby City of Troy appeared to manage quite well with a volunteer department.

Falling Fruits

In either event, the *Oakland Press,* in an editorial written by one-time editor Neil Munro, informed its readers that Pontiac's "border war" was far from over.

Recognizing that the Silverdome was in the City of Pontiac, but that its adjacent property that appeared ripe for development was in the township, he noted many in the city would like to see the land in question become part of the city which would then enable the city to gain tax revenues generated therein.

After all, many felt, the city had "risked its neck" developing the Silverdome and was therefore entitled to benefit from such newly emerging tax dollars.

"Why," Munro rhetorically asked, "should these stadium 'fruits' fall on the Township side of the fence?"

In the township, many others asked, "Why not?"

Munro summed it up succinctly: "The battle lines are drawn."

At issue was simply a chunk of Silverdome parking lot. But larger annexation threats clouded the horizon, the Opdyke corridor horizon that is.

Munro noted the Boundary Commission was saddled "with playing Solomon" in such cases like these in which municipal boundaries go right through the middle of areas which really are one, not two, economic units.

He summarized the dilemma faced by the commission in the City of Pontiac—Pontiac Township dispute:

Should Pontiac Township become yet another small Oakland County city "cheek by jowl" with an existing one?

Could the Township—as a township—adequately serve the enormous amount of development that was expected along its western boundary?

Could the Township survive economically—as a township or a city—if it loses that potential development area and accompanying rich tax income to the City of Pontiac?

Or, though the question hadn't been officially asked, should all of the township become part of the City of Pontiac?

Munro's fine sense of local history was evident in his appraisal of the situation at the time.

"Forty years ago, the Township could have been annexed to the City with scarcely a word of protest," he wrote with great credibility. "But now it has developed some 'identity' of its own and Pontiac does not have the positive, prosperous image it had in the past."

Munro clarified the larger picture by acknowledging that even if the Boundary Commission said Pontiac Township should be a city, citizens there could still petition to put the issue on the ballot and reject it. Incorporation would also be rejected if citizens failed to adopt a charter within two years or actually rejected two proposed charters. Furthermore, any decisions could be challenged in the courts.

On February 8, 1978, township officials cheered and clapped as the State Boundary Commission decided to allow township residents to vote on incorporation.

"Our people have sat here for years," Grusnick said that day. "Now is the time development is coming. Our people ought to get the dividends."

Grusnick predicted incorporation would spur development and help bring in more federal grants.

Boundary Commission decision making was complicated by the presence of a group of local landowners who were organized as "the Opdyke Corridor Corporation," an ad hoc consortium of interests who, among other things, expressed the opinion their properties would bring higher value if those properties were part of the City of Pontiac.

The State Boundary Commission, at its meeting of April 19, 1978, approved the proposed incorporation of part of Pontiac Township into a new home-rule city. The commission also ordered a special election of nine charter commissioners. Pontiac Township became the Charter Township of Pontiac as an interim measure against annexation.

On January 9, 1979, the following resolution was adopted by the State Boundary Commission:

> *Whereas, the State Boundary Commission meeting in Lansing, Michigan, on April 19, 1978, approved the proposed incorporation of part of Pontiac Township into a new home city, and*
>
> *Whereas, no petition asking for an election on the question has been filed as authorized . . .*
>
> *Therefore be it resolved that: The Boundary Commission orders a special election for the election of nine charter commissioners to be held on September 11, 1979, and be it further resolved that: Charter commission candidates must be electors of the proposed new city and must file non-partisan candidate petitions containing the signatures of 20 qualified electors residing in the proposed municipality with the Oakland County Clerk no later than July 23, 1979.*

It was further resolved that the State Boundary Commission prescribe the ballot form. And so it turned out that Docket No. 77-I-1 was on its way to changing the course of (local) history.

The election for charter commissioners was held September 11, 1979, and the elected individuals were

- Dorothy A. Babb (763 votes)
- Helen M. Boone (688 votes)
- Michael Craig Davis (679 votes)
- Robert W. Grusnick (934 votes)
- Walter G. Smith (711 votes)
- Helen R. Baum (681 votes)
- Joe L. Carter (614 votes)
- E. Dale Fisk (748 votes)
- Henry V. Knight (582 votes)

The first meeting of the charter commission was held October 4, 1979. All commissioners were present.

The oath of office was administered by the township clerk. Eventually, twenty-nine meetings were held concerning the charter.

The next step was to elect a chairman. After four votes, the venerable and highly energized Dale Fisk was elected to this important position.

The charter was made up of several sections. The main sections were

1. Form of government
2. Mill rates
3. Proposed new city name
4. Time and date to take effect

Chairman Fisk instructed Secretary Helen Baum to notify the State Boundary Commission that a first meeting had been held.

One week later, the new board convened again and met Don Oakes. He explained to the commission that he had written sixteen charters, and that all but four had been adopted. Oakes advised that where responsibility is placed is very important in the organization of government.

Oakes said there were two types of organizations: legislative (which is policy making) and administrative, which is the handling of day-to-day functions.

Questions lingered. Would they opt for a city manager form or a strong mayor type of government?

Only in a charter, Oakes instructed, could the strong mayor/weak mayor issue be resolved. By meeting on a weekly basis, he advised members they would complete their charter within six months. The group did meet regularly throughout this time period although lapses of two or three weeks were common.

On November 14, 1979, an important motion made by Commissioner Dorothy Babb was passed. It called for the establishment of a three-person subcommittee to make the public aware of the progress of the charter commission and to also solicit input for a new name for the nascent community.

Options were discussed regarding the future of the Village of Lake Angelus. Four alternatives existed:

- Become part of the proposed city
- Annex to the Township of Waterford
- Annex to the City of Pontiac
- Become a city or township of its own

Lake Angelus eventually opted for incorporation as a city.

By now, the commission was getting down to brass tacks.

Issues like a preamble, boundaries, general municipal powers, and intergovernmental cooperation began to dominate meeting agenda.

By December 5, consensus was achieved that Oakes should draw up a proposed charter on the assumption that it would be a council/manager type of government.

In early 1980, concrete considerations were being nailed down on a regular basis, addressing subpoints like nomination procedures, terms of office, approval of petitions, and forms of ballots. Letters were sent to various civic-minded organizations in the community, requesting time at one of their meetings to update residents on the future of their local government.

Wringing their hands over the most miniscule of all imaginable questions and concerns, commissioners busied themselves through the winter, examining details and nuances and holding every conceivable consideration up to the light in order to fully examine its efficacy.

Portions were deleted from ordinances after ponderous soul-searching with the invaluable Oakes chiming in on a regular basis.

Given his involvement in this telling phase, it seems obvious the consultant earned his $35-per-hour fees, including driving time to and from his home in the Grand Rapids area.

Origin of the Name of Auburn Hills

After the charter commission was elected and the charter was written, it became important to establish a name for the new city.

In fact, a "name void" of sorts had lingered for eons, inhibiting progress decidedly yet also in a subtle, unspoken way perceptible only to fervent observers of this specific drama.

The name "Pontiac Heights" was most commonly evoked during this time frame. It resonated, but not audibly.

Voices of persuasion from the business community formed something of a chorus in suggesting that dropping the name "Pontiac" would probably be propitious for residents who were about to be impacted by coming changes.

"We were advised by many insurance and investment firms that, if we dropped the name 'Pontiac' from our official name, we would probably enjoy some benefits for the people of our community," Mike Davis wrote.

These benefits included lower insurance premiums, better interest rates from companies "who might not know the area but only the name 'Pontiac' which at the time was struggling to fight crime, overcome budget constraints, and maintain political integrity."

The "upside" of retaining a muted Pontiac identity was obvious to everyone: it removed any ambiguity as to the location of the emerging new city.

In leveraging their geographic proximity to the surrounding-on-two-sides city, this fledging entity could achieve immediate front-of-mind awareness.

The "downside" was equally evident: any association with Pontiac also brought with it a risk of confusing identities with the full mix of difficulties the city was experiencing due to reductions in automotive industry-related aging industries and other salient stress points.

Davis was right. As it sought to fight crime, experienced lapses in its infrastructures, adjusted to continued waves of budget reductions, and worked to overcome perceptions of deterioration in political integrity, the city named after a famous Indian chief had become, by the late twentieth century, somewhat less than luminous.

It's also worth noting that Meadowbrook, as a name and a point of enduring identity, almost stuck.

But as Davis pointed out, Meadowbrook brought with it too much potential for confusion—or perhaps convulsion—for it to have ever succeeded in this all-important exercise in name selection.

Fearful of clashing identities with such a significant enterprise as a mall with that name, officials went back to the drawing board for additional ideas.

Many wanted to keep the name "Auburn Heights."

It had been the unofficial name of the small part of the southern portion of the township. The main problem with that strategy was that taking that course risked alienating the northern portion of the city on the rise, particularly those forward-thinking souls who lived north of Hamlin Road.

Opinions swirled all over the map.

Commission members continued to revert to keeping the name Auburn in the discussion mix.

After all, the name Auburn Heights had originated from the City of Auburn, New York, by early settlers who clearly inferred similarities in the graceful blend of hardwoods that dominated early landscapes in the area.

On the flipside of the discussion, others felt the choice of name should also demonstrate to insiders and outsiders alike that *something had changed* in old Pontiac Township.

Further contemplation ensued.

Much head scratching occurred, and the imagination of an entire community became bent upon this important exercise in choosing a handle. Adept area researchers came upon a realization of galactic significance: heights and hills are basically the same, in inference and in fact.

A mailing was sent out to the community to seek names for the new city. More than eight hundred township residents were challenged to help in the process. The name that emerged most consistently from that mailing was Meadowbrook. It wasn't going to work.

"Some on the Charter Commission were concerned because a new indoor mall has just been built in the nearby Rochester area that was called the Meadowbrook Mall," Davis wrote. "Fearing that we might lose some identity, a different name was discussed."

Getting the name right proved to be a laborious process. Stated otherwise, finding what *would* work proved to be the most vexing undertaking.

In addition to tax questions and the matter of how much power to entrust to the city manager, charter commissioners had spent months contemplating the challenge of choosing a new name.

As the hour for the final vote on the issue approached, commission members sat silently, keeping their thoughts to themselves.

Then Commissioner Davis broke the ice.

"I urge you to reconsider the name 'Meadowbrook.' It's a pretty word but I think if we use it, we'd be making a grave error. I don't honestly believe the charter will pass if we use 'Meadowbrook.'"

Davis's remark began to turn the tide. The commission had already considered between twenty and thirty names for the new city. But now suddenly they appeared ready to consider a few more.

Township Treasurer Dorothy Babb threw out the name "Clinton Corner."

Supervisor Grusnick produced a similarly unlikely one, "Squirrel Creek."

Neither offering inspired much enthusiasm.

Another name did—the City of Auburn Hills.

Accounts vary as to whom exactly first evoked the name.

By most accounts, it was either Mike Davis or Henry Knight. Even official minutes from charter commission meetings lack complete clarity on the question. So getting to the bottom of it will have to be left to future historians.

History *should* show that both Davis *and* Knight played enormous roles in shaping the destiny of their community.

So whether both or just one of them said it, the question was asked, "How about 'Auburn Hills'?"

Whoever said it nailed it.

"I believe it's a good compromise and a name that carries over the idea of Auburn Heights," Knight commented *that night*.

A man in the audience, Harold Burmeister, agreed.

"I'd like to see a new name and get the feeling of a new start," he said.

And that was that. Once again, momentum seized the moment in the nascent city, proving once again that anytime you combine moment and unstoppable movement you're liable to experience sheer synergy.

In an instant, the commissioners voted 5-2 to approve the idea of changing their proposed city's name from Meadowbrook to Auburn Hills.

And so was born the name Auburn Hills.

At last, a name was conceived, applauded, fallen in love with, and ultimately blessed by every interested party in sight.

Early political leaders heaved a collective sigh of relief. Hallelujah, a name had appeared in their minds that represented a little of the old and a little of the new and brought "North and South" together, where they were destined to remain for time immemorial.

Auburn: Truly "of" the Hills

It would be wrong to think that in adding a *Hills* connotation, commissioners were seeking in any way to imply any association with, say, the nearby Bloomfield Hills, home to millionaires, screen stars, famous soul singers, filthy rich computer geeks, and auto industry icons amuck.

No, that was not going to happen in deliriously modest Auburn—whatever its name was.

The legend of Pontiac Township is deeply rooted in basic values and friendly, neighborly mentality. As a matter of fact, those ethics continue to define what it is that gives this place, among others, its appeal and true identity.

For the record, the presumptuous act of adding *Hills* to city names was fairly prevalent in Oakland County back in the good old twentieth century, because of the undulating nature of the earth supporting it.

Retreating glaciers that heaved all of nature beneath them as they rumbled back toward Hudson Bay about twenty thousand years ago when Oakland County assumed its current shape had divined this quadrant of Southeast Michigan topsy-turvy indeed, especially along a line that extends across the northeastern portion of Oakland County.

There is no flat land in Auburn Hills or any of the communities with the word *hills* in it in Oakland County. Everything undulates, even attention spans.

Farmington Hills, Beverly Hills, and eventually Rochester Hills were all incarnations inspired by topography. Auburn Hills came to this party at its own pace but with equal acceptability in the realm of appropriate choice of name.

No, some nefarious band of coconspirators did not manufacture the "hills" concept in order to attach false pulchritude to the new city. Rather, Auburn was always of the hills—distinctly so.

Auburn Hills also eventually became one of about 3,100 towns, cities, and counties in America that has adopted policies that seek to encourage planting and coexisting with trees in order to improve air quality, moderate temperature, dampen noise, and provide shade according to the National Arbor Day Foundation.

Legalisms Beget Optimism

On August 12, 1980, Township Attorney James P. Sheehy wrote to City of Pontiac Attorney Thomas E. Hunter regarding pending litigation between the two governmental entities.

Sheehy's letter acknowledged various discussions and court appearances regarding the case. The court suggested the two parties resolve their conflicts out of court. Considering the fact the then Charter Township of Pontiac had presently pending the process of incorporation.

A charter was being formed that would be voted upon by residents. "Should the voters of the Township approve the incorporation, the boundaries of the new City would exclude the six acres which are the subject of (its) lawsuit," Sheehy wrote.

"I suggest that the city council rescind their action of annexation so as to return the six acres legally to the position the property was in prior to annexation."

Sheehy further recommended that the township board, upon becoming a city, take formal actions to grant the City of Pontiac said six acres.

"I personally believe that it is in the best interest of both communities to work in the spirit of cooperation in resolving this dispute," he continued. "I further believe that if this settlement can be properly arranged that it will strengthen the communication between the Charter Township of Pontiac and the City of Pontiac."

Days later, Supervisor Grusnick replied by letter to Sheehy, indicating the matter needed to be discussed with the township board prior to any commitment being made.

Hunter subsequently replied, indicating his legal team had discussed the issue with the Pontiac City Commission. He questioned the proposition of the City of Pontiac rescinding the 1977 annexation and relying on the township to turn over the six acres at a later date.

In essence, the City of Pontiac indicated it was less than convinced such an offer would later become binding on an as yet undetermined governmental entity. Given those considerations, Hunter suggested a consent judgment be entered "to the effect that the matter be held in its current status by the (Circuit) Court until the present incorporation effort in the Township be resolved."

In response to Hunter's letter, Sheehy wrote Grusnick saying although he, Sheehy, did not agree with Hunter's approach to resolving the impasse, he felt it was worth continuing the dialogue "in an attempt to reach a friendly solution to this matter."

On April 7, 1981, township voters were asked to approve or disapprove incorporation. On that day, they voted on a lengthy charter that established the basis of a new form of government. If a charter was approved, city officials would then be elected and city government would become official.

Township government would be dismantled, replaced by a form of city government. A city manager would run the ship rather than the current supervisor, and a mayor would head the city council.

Grusnick said in the days leading up to the historic vote, he saw incorporation as the only way to protect "the integrity" of the township and "its investment in water and sewer service to the area of the proposed sports arena."

The proposed arena had been dubbed as "Olympia II" and was to have been built across Opdyke Road from the Pontiac Silverdome. It was supposedly going to become the new home for the Detroit Red Wings hockey team although—quite incredibly—it never came to be.

The arena would have ostensibly triggered a growth explosion in its vicinity. History shows that amazing spurt of development took place without this particular facility, however nicely it may have fit into the scheme of things.

For the record, the "new" hockey arena considered for Oakland County was later named Joe Louis Arena and was built on the shores on the Detroit River instead of in the middle of Mayor Young's frequently derided "cornfields" of Pontiac Township.

As voters contemplated their priorities and wishes in the days leading up to the crucial date of April 7, annexation efforts by the City of Pontiac remained in litigation.

A petition bearing the names of 1,200 township residents had been filed requesting incorporation in late 1977. Grusnick had delivered the signatures himself.

In March 1978, the application was approved and a charter commission had subsequently been elected and given a mandate of writing a detailed proposal for incorporation. That document was approved in early 1981.

At this time, there were already more than seventy cities in Southeast Michigan, of more than 230 independent municipalities.

On April 7, 1981, the new city charter was approved by the electorate. Of 1,796 votes cast, the "Yes" votes tallied 1,215; "No" votes were 581.

The rest is history, profound history.

The name "the City of Auburn Hills" was chosen providing final resolution to the "Heights vs. Hills" discussion, dispelling any references to "Amy" or "township."

The past was relegated to antiquity. The future was set in motion, there to redefine what had been with what was destined to become.

Michigan Secretary of State Richard H. Austin on September 1, 1983, certified in the document above that

> *the attached verified description of territory in the Charter Township of Pontiac, Oakland County, was approved by the State Boundary Commission under the provisions of Act 191, Public Acts of 1968, as amended, for incorporation as a home rule city; I further certify documents on file in this office indicate a charter for the City of Auburn Hills was adopted at an election held on April 7, 1981; I further certify that on December 31, 1983, at 1:00 p.m. the City of Auburn Hills, Oakland County, Michigan, becomes a duly incorporated home rule city operating under the provisions of Act 279, Public Acts of 1909, as amended; and I further certify the area incorporated contains approximately 17.2 square miles with a 1980 census figure of approximately 15,388, a population density of approximately 894.65 inhabitants per square mile.*

The first city council was elected in 1983, and the City of Auburn Hills was inaugurated December 31, 1983.

During the period leading up to the proposed adoption of the charter, concerns emerged from the City of Pontiac, the Township of Orion, and the Village of Lake Angelus.

The City of Pontiac wrote a letter to the State Boundary Commission in which it cited content from an in-house economic study. Pontiac's allegations were rebuffed with gusto by township officials.

The City of Pontiac also contacted the township attorney regarding the annexation case and indicated that they hoped it might go away.

In spite of these occurrences it was determined the issues at hand would be resolved only after the vote on the charter.

Orion Township officials indicated they were concerned that the new city would be in effect annexing the area around the General Motors Orion assembly plant in the area of Brown and Giddings roads.

As for the Village of Lake Angelus, township officials asked if they wanted to be included as a part of the new city; they declined, indicating they wanted to maintain their own governmental autonomy.

By 1983, government officials and legal representatives had agreed upon and ironed out the details regarding a mutual consent resolution concerning property annexed from Pontiac Charter Township to Village of Lake Angelus, which in effect represented the final phase of intercommunity discussions and actions related to incorporation efforts in the area.

The charter commission met on July 23, 1980, and set the date and time that the charter would take effect, agreeing on December 31, 1983, at 1:00 PM. A certificate that affirmed this action was received from the Michigan secretary of state.

Discussion of what form of government was limited and consensus was easily achieved. The "Council Manager" form of government was blessed at a special meeting conducted in April 1980.

In December of that year, the mills for operation were established as follows:

- General Fund—Not less than one mill, not more than two mills
- Fire Fund—Not less than half a mill, not more than two mills
- Police Fund—Not less than six mills, not more than eight and a half mills

The mills were to be assessed against each $1,000 of valuation. On November 8, 1981, the citizens voted the following individuals to the first city council:

- Michael C. Davis
- Dale Fisk

- David Jerrell
- Walter G. Smith
- Larry G. Douglas
- Robert W. Grusnick
- Ronald Shirley

The vote on incorporation

As the vote on incorporation approached, no one could predict the outcome. It was far from certain whether Michigan would end up with one less township and one more city. Opposition to the idea had not surfaced to any meaningful extent. But nothing was absolutely predictable.

Significant support of the concept of incorporation was also notably absent. If anyone was actively promoting the idea, that impact failed to excite the average observer.

Those who could have most logically taken on that responsibility—the members of the commission who drafted the proposed City of Auburn Hills Charter—had instead adapted a role of providing pro and con information to township residents and otherwise staying out of any other potential source of controversy.

Over fifty residents per night had responded to the information sessions commission members staged about the township. The discussions had been thorough, spicy, and centered on basic questions.

To the surprise of no one, questions regarding taxes dominated. Once appraised of what commission members said would be an essential continuation of the township's then current tax rate, most residents in attendance appeared to be in support of the notion of incorporation.

Commission members continued to cite the possibility of future annexation attempts on the township from the City of Pontiac as the principle rationale for adopting incorporation.

Even though the City of Pontiac was losing its clout in many respects, this argument resonated deeply within the community.

Technically at least, the annexation threat existed unless township residents opted for incorporation.

It's Official!

The first meeting of the new city council was held under a large tent in the parking lot at 1827 N. Squirrel Road on the last business day of 1983.

The temperature on that day dipped into the deeply frigid below zero range. Legend has it those who attended were pleased when the ceremonies were over.

The agenda was as follows:

- Rev. Richard Chilkott from the Gloria Dei Church offered the opening prayer.
- National and state flags were presented and attendees recited the Pledge of Allegiance.
- The meeting was called to order by E. Dale Fisk, who asked former township clerk Veronica New to call the roll of the new council members.
- Plaques were presented to the city charter members

    o E. Dale Fisk
    o Dorothy Babb
    o Robert W. Grusnick
    o Michael Davis
    o Henry Knight
    o Walter Smith
    o Joe Carter
    o Helen Boone
    o Helen Venos

- Rev. William Palmer, pastor of the Auburn Heights United Presbyterian Church, presented the invocation.
- Presentations were made by the Hill-Gazette Post No. 143 of the American Legion and the supervisor of Orion Township.
- Mayor Wallace Holland from the City of Pontiac was introduced and extended congratulations from his city.

Other dignitaries in attendance were

- Oakland County Executive Dan Murphy
- Oakland County Clerk Lynn Allen
- Michigan State Representative Rudi Nichols

Representative Nichols said he hoped that the new City of Auburn Hills would continue with "the enthusiasm generated by the Township and rise to even greater heights which he knew the city was capable of," according to an account in the Jan. 2, 1984, issue of the *Auburn Hills Community News*.

Representatives from nearby townships, school districts, Oakland Community College, and Oakland University also took part.

Mr. Fisk thanked the Boy Scouts and Girl Scouts for their help in setting up the chairs and various other jobs they undertook.

The election of officers was conducted.

Robert W. Grusnick, who had served as township supervisor, was elected as first mayor of the City of Auburn Hills.

Walter Smith was elected as the first mayor pro tem.

The mayor was only a ceremonial title. As such, the mayor only had authority to conduct meetings.

The job of running the day-to-day operations of the new city was turned over to the police chief Robert Raynor who fulfilled the city manager function until a full-time professional was hired.

Acting as new mayor, Grusnick stated that because the new council had been meeting since the election on November 8, 1983, he felt the transition would be smooth.

Veronica New was appointed city clerk and Dorothy Babb as treasurer of the new city. All existing department heads were retained.

After a few other items of business, the meeting was adjourned, the closing prayer being offered by Rev. Gordon C. Lindsay, pastor of the Five Points Community Church.

Following the ceremonies, speechmaking, and other histrionics, refreshments were served *inside* the city hall.

Part 2

A City Takes Identity

A City Takes Identity

The City of Auburn Hills was officially convened in 1983, just in time to become the city it was already fast becoming.

In many respects, the wagon was truly pulling the horse.

If the new City of Auburn Hills had not already become a city when it did, it would have had to do so eventually, sooner than later as things turned out.

With the passage of time in the late twentieth century, there was no holding back the surge of commercial growth that was about to well up along Opdyke Road, in the rich-in-potential acres connecting Oakland University along the I-75 corridor and throughout the archaic township.

Whether the formality of incorporation hastened what would follow in the way of jaw-dropping commercial development is merely an academic question now, something for all the professors at Oakland University to kick around.

Yes or no, it's probably not an important consideration, given the momentum already surging through the hills hereabouts, the spirit unloosed in the ribbon of humanity that occupied the former rural territory immediately east and north of the City of Pontiac.

Voters in the former Pontiac Township had agreed to give cityhood a try. Few of them could have foreseen what came next, an explosion of corporate presence perhaps unequaled at any time in the late twentieth century anywhere in the Midwest.

On December 31, 1983, a small community known as Pontiac Township became the City of Auburn Hills.

This single event set in motion a succession of undertakings that, seen in the aggregate many decades later, amounts to nothing short of unprecedented redefinition.

Where dirt roads once ruled rose larger-than-life, state-of-the-art office buildings, concrete, steel, and glass configurations of the highest order.

Skyscrapers, many architecturally amazing, shot up in clusters and pockets from Orion to Rochester. Quite staggeringly, they restructured what anyone perceived to be the logical parameters of the Greater Detroit area or the radical new aura of Auburn whatever it had been before it started becoming what it eventually became.

Bold and splendidly designed buildings replaced nothingness in the former mist, manifesting in multiples, some of them nearly touching the clouds, appearing here and there all at once, sprouting into the sky atop hills, aside ravines, fording creeks and crevices, recasting the essence of ambient nature aside the mighty concrete shores of vital transportation arteries called M-59 and I-75, recasting everything within the primal paths of commerce.

Onlookers slapped their foreheads in mock disbelief as society beheld widescale transformation so vast it seemed unimaginable *even as it occurred*.

Tidiness and taste seized the moment. If rate of growth alone was not enough to stretch the ability of the average thinking person's brain to even conceive such change, the poetic order that characterized the birth of this city on the make was even more auspicious.

An entirely new face was imposed upon the physical landscape, yet it occurred so gracefully and without offense it was almost as if it didn't happen at all. Or if it did, the improvements were so appealing they merely enhanced the already sublime.

Total Tax Values Tell the Story

Reviewing the City of Auburn Hills's tax base history, it's apparent the increase in total tax value from 1978 until 2005 in the one-time bucolic township was so dramatic and beyond conventional statistical experience it had to be explained in this context, in terms that make sense to people of common intelligence.

You might want to clean the lens on your reading glasses before going any further as the numbers you will encounter are entirely outside the range of conventional believability.

Tax figures typically defy average comprehension. They're just numbers on a page, hard to interpret and subject to instant confusion. Having established that, please note the following numerical summation of what happened to the overall tax base in this community is both true and outside the scope of normal imagination.

From 1978 until 2005, what happened in the new City of Auburn Hills was so overwhelming, only indisputable digital definition does the subject justice. Some years—1986 and 1999 specifically—the rate of increase was as high as a mind-boggling 32 percent.

Let the record show, 1986 marked the time when construction began on both the Palace of Auburn Hills and the Chrysler Technology Center; 1999 is when the Great Lakes Crossing Mall was built and opened, triggering large retail development in its formidable shadows.

In a world where 5-percent growth is noteworthy, 32-percent growth is incomprehensible and outside the range of plausibility. Yet it happened, twice. The 32-percent reference is not a typographical error.

Another way to say 32 percent is one-third. One-third of anything is almost half of it and pretty close to all of it. In other words, Auburn Hills nearly doubled in value two different times in its first decade of existence.

For a municipality—or any entity for that matter—to grow at a rate of one-third in one year is unprecedented. That it happened TWICE in Auburn Hills reveals growth patterns virtually unexperienced anywhere outside the Sunbelt or possibly Tokyo or Dubai, just possibly.

From the late 1970s to the mid-2000s Auburn Hills went from tiny to gigantic as measured by its tax base.

Overall, the total tax value in 1978 was approximately $177,000,000. By 2005 that figure had increased to $5,000,000,000, going from the relatively low millions to the lofty billions.

The difference between less than 200 million and 5 billion—whether measured in dollars or yen or corn futures—is the same as having two or twenty-five marbles in your bag, assuming the person doing *this* math still has any marbles of his own.

From the time of its incorporation to the twenty-five-year anniversary of that occasion, the city had expanded its purview so dramatically it had become nearly impossible to recall its humble origins.

Only in visiting city offices at 1827 N. Squirrel Road could a visitor perhaps conjure again memories of an era past, before the world came to its door and major entertainment and corporate presences settled into the neighborhood.

Known now as the Civic Center, the pristine acres that accommodate city offices and departments are the site of the former estate of millionaire real estate developer Wesson Seyburn, husband of Winifred Dodge, the oldest child of John F. Dodge. Seyburn once used the estate as a weekend getaway.

The city acquired the property in late 1976 from developer Sam Frankel for $142,000. Administrators and workers moved into the new facility from the old town hall at 2060 Opdyke Road.

Since that time, there have been modifications to the property and its buildings. What was once a barn and horse stables became the city's administrative offices. An old carriage house became the council chambers. The mansion morphed into the community center.

As a result of the city preserving the buildings on the campus, Auburn Hills has been able to maintain its old-fashioned charm.

The tastefully remodeled structures that comprised the old Seyburn Estate remain to this date evocative statements connecting the charming past and the bold future with their elegant wooden treatments, open views, and country ambience.

Quiet conviviality also continues to define the interpersonal motif in these surroundings. Smiling and dignified public servants inhabit airy work-stations projecting efficiency and Northern hospitality.

Not everything changed around here, just almost everything.

Auburn Hills Leads Oakland County Transformation

Of course, Oakland County was changing just as quickly as the City of Auburn Hills, particularly in the final two decades of the twentieth century.

From 1983 to 1988, Michigan gained 538,000 new jobs—the fourth largest net job increase of any state in the nation. Most of those jobs came to the tri-county area comprising metropolitan Detroit, with Oakland County the primary driver of job growth according to then director of Michigan's Department of Commerce, Doug Ross.

"Pontiac is situated in the middle of one of the biggest boom areas in America," Ross said at the time.

Ross said Oakland County was adding "world-class" industry—industry that operates in an international marketplace. These firms created a demand for skilled local people and at the same time serve as "a magnet" for skilled people from around the world.

Oakland County—and, increasingly, the new City of Auburn Hills—became home to 40 percent of the nation's robotics industry and to 40 percent of Michigan's top 50 high-tech companies.

Economic growth continued to accelerate in the early 1990s as new activities began generating in and around the 1,800-acre Oakland Technology Park in Auburn Hills. Billions of dollars in new business development and tens of thousands of new jobs accompanied this dramatic movement.

The technology park operates in conjunction with nearby Oakland University; the two exchange educational programs, research, and technology.

Chrysler Technology Center became an anchor tenant in the technology park in the early 1990s. It purchased five hundred acres in the Oakland Technology Park and proceeded to construct a $2 billion three-million-square-foot technology center.

Other major players in the development were

- Comerica Bank
- Electronic Data Systems
- GMF Robotics
- Schostak Brothers & Company

In addition, each of Detroit's Big Three automotive manufacturers set up technological research centers in the complex that also became home to a plethora of international automotive supplier firms.

Joe Joachim, then director of Oakland County's Department of Community and Economic Development, said momentum for basing such a concentration of automotive-based business interests in the Auburn Hills area was a direct result of the early 1980s recession.

"General Motors, Ford, and Chrysler began telling their suppliers they had to get more competitive with the imports," Joachim said at the time.

"They were getting leaner and meaner, skimming back overhead, and beginning to outsource functions like research, development, and engineering to this new structure of supplier industries they'd created where suppliers are chosen in terms of their cost effectiveness and quality," Joachim said.

"It all sprouted up from what were just before sales offices for these suppliers."

Soon they were offering engineering and research as well.

Joachim continued. "The Big Three said, 'Do it close to home.' So the companies grew right here in Oakland County. Companies like ITT, Dupont, General Electric . . . doubled in size and increased their research activities. When it came to outsourcing, the Big Three found a highly qualified technical labor pool in their own backyard. This is where all the knowledge is . . . the talent to help these companies become more competitive."

In the early 1980s, then Michigan Governor William Milliken had established a high technology task force and empowered its representatives to identify possible locations for intensive development of high-technology, high-growth industries.

Within a year, a representative from the Department of Commerce attended a meeting where he met Joseph Champagne, then president of Oakland University, and the two struck up a conversation. Soon, the topic turned to possible industrial development opportunities, and the men agreed to spend further time together exploring the land surrounding the university.

"It all clicked at that meeting," Champagne later said. "We were talking about land use and industrial development, and I thought, hey, what about putting some type of research development here near Oakland University and the I-75 corridor where we already have thousands of acres of land, existing gas lines, railroad tracks across M-59, a river running through, water mains in and everything here, along with the university.

"I thought, my god, dummy Joe, look what you have right here in your own backyard."

By 1983, the view from those vistas included the emerging Oakland Technology Park led by Comerica.

Overall, the pace of development in the 1,500-plus-acre park was a source of amazement for local political officials.

The Auburn Hills city manager at the time, Leonard Hendricks, said 65 percent of the buildings that would ultimately comprise the Oakland Technology Park were already in place by 1989.

"What was supposed to be a twenty-year development scenario became more like a ten-year scenario," he said. "Nobody knew it would be of this magnitude, and nobody knew it would happen this fast.'

Auburn Hills: A City is Born

Development of Auburn Hills stretched from the southeast corner of the city, near the GMF Robotics facility in Rochester Hills, all the way north to the front yard of the GM Orion plant in Orion Township.

Along its route, a dazzling extension of stunning new office and research buildings began to dot nearly every intersection and hillside. The emphasis at most of these modern new facilities was on robotics, computer operations, engineering automation, and advanced manufacturing applications.

The area also became the address of several hotels, office buildings, and research and engineering facilities. Over a hundred new buildings—most of them a hundred thousand square feet or larger—were almost instantly nestled throughout Auburn Hills.

Clusters of new offices and research facilities sit atop hills beside flowing rivers, in groves of protected walnut trees, and alongside obscure roads that until the late 1980s were unpaved vestiges of a time when townships were still townships and potholes reigned supreme.

Bob Grusnick, the city's first mayor and the former township supervisor, said the dramatic development of the Oakland Technology Park occurred as a result of the efforts of the coalition comprised of Champagne and representatives of Comerica, Schostak Brothers, Oakland Community College, and primarily landowners in the area.

He said the growth of Oakland Technology Park also gathered momentum when the voters of then Pontiac Township voted to adopt incorporation and change the name of the community in the early 1980s.

"That had a big impact," he said. "I don't think we would have seen all this growth . . . to this extent . . . without those changes. Now we've gone from having dew in the grass to having cushioning in our beds."

The numbers supported Grusnick's statement: Auburn Hills's assessed property value nearly tripled, from $131 million in 1984 to $330 million in 1989; and the number of people working in the city increased from 4,000 in 1980 to 16,000 in 1990.

The Oakland Technology Park emerged as a major jobs generator over the years based on studies conducted by the University of Michigan for the Southeast Michigan Council of Governments (SEMCOG). As of 1990, buildings under construction or completed in and around the park totaled 9.4 million square feet of floor area.

"It's becoming a center of technology, which I don't think is going to be repeated anywhere in the Midwest," Joe Joachim said at the time.

"It firmly establishes Oakland County as being the technology center of this region."

Auburn Hills Cast in Bold New Light

Four primary occurrences convened on the new City of Auburn Hills in its early years, completing the dramatic reinventing of a place in time, a township-turned-city enveloped in rarified destiny.

The stunning Palace of Auburn Hills and the Chrysler Technology Center and corporate headquarters—the second largest office building in America (after the Pentagon)—came in the late 1980s.

Almost simultaneously the newly minted Automation Alley imparted major identity along the I-75 Corridor, through Auburn Hills and up and down the trajectory of the vital interstate highway.

Then, ten years later, a reality-changing mall of all malls arose in the northern portions of the new city—the entirely incomprehensible Great Lakes Crossing—and all surrounding retail explosion set in motion in its periphery.

With the emergence of the Palace, the bold Chrysler campus, Automation Alley, and Great Lakes Crossing, Auburn Hills assumed an entirely new identity.

Four manifestations secured a new city's status and standing, turned a once kicked back township on its head, created a foundation of assured prosperity, and cast an entirely new face on an already appealing slice of civilization.

Here is the upshot, one observer's "take," on who and what drove these occurrences in informal and somewhat subjective tonality.

The Palace of Auburn Hills

In 1986, construction began for the Palace of Auburn Hills on a sixty-five-acre site at 3777 Lapeer Road; opening night was celebrated August 13, 1988.

Everything changed after that. Once a mere vision in a few people's imagination, it became one of the American Midwest's leading premier entertainment and sports venues. Out of nowhere, it became the glitziest destination in Southeast Michigan.

Knowing the Palace of Auburn Hills rose from a barren field in the late 1980s is to fully appreciate the significance of its emergence journey back a few decades to 1974, when William Davidson bought the Detroit Pistons professional basketball team from Fred Zollner for $8 million.

By most accounts, Davidson perceived the franchise as something resembling a minor lark in his larger existence.

However, as a driven, results-oriented industrialist/philanthropist/businessman, it was Davidson's nature to pursue excellence, perfection, and a command competitive presence.

This fledging National Basketball Association franchise became the vehicle that would drive Davidson and associates to unthinkable levels of success.

"Maybe a year after I bought the team and had the idea it was going to be fun, I realized it was a business," Davidson told the *Detroit Free Press*. "So then I began to conduct it as a business. We tried to make it into a model franchise."

Established in Fort Wayne, Indiana, in 1941-42, the Pistons moved to Detroit for the 1957-58 season.

They not only bounced around various Detroit stadiums, they actually scheduled a playoff game at the Grosse Pointe High School gym in 1960 when no other facility was available. Other major asterisks accompany the sometimes-bizarre history of the franchise. On one quaint evening during the 1985-86 season, a collapsed roof at the Silverdome caused the team to retreat to Joe Louis Arena to play game 5 of a key playoff series.

In all, the team played in seven different buildings in the Detroit area before moving into the Palace.

It happened in the late 1980s when legions of construction cranes stood like majestic towers across the broad plains at I-75 and Lapeer Road, begetting an arena so spectacular and well conceived even the smuggest skeptic had to bury the cynicism, set down the clipboard, and cheer out loud.

From 1986-88, it was as if a large egg had been hatched in the apex of Auburn Hills, giving birth to a humongous project that surged to rapid maturity as a multipurpose sports/entertainment complex. A mega-arena of such breathtaking magnificence, it illumined suburban skies casting a new light across the universe as locally defined.

The Palace of Auburn Hills was so majestic, so sweetly designed and realized, so mightily magnificent in size and overall construction, that the sudden reality of its new presence enlivened the entire surrounding area with its splendor. Clearly, its luster imposed gentility and excitement upon the entire region and the excellence of its expression not only raised the bar, it closed the bar and was there to help open it the next morning.

It is entirely possible the rhetoric is excessive. Then again, the writer could just as easily be understating what happened when Bill Davidson told his development group to think big, think gorgeous and extravagant and excitement, and build an arena worthy of hosting one of the NBA's hottest up-and-coming franchises.

During that brief period, during that surge of particular construction in the late 1980s, the world's awareness of Auburn Hills underwent permanent change of radical proportion. From obscure to preeminent, Auburn Hills cascaded on global consciousness as a fully uptown embodiment of glitz, class, and mainstream taste.

People went from never hearing of this place to literally hearing way too much about it. And much of this occurred, we should add, simply as a result of the arrival of one stunning arena in the suburbs, in the heart of audacious Auburn Hills.

Named in a public-conducted contest to put a moniker on a new sporting venue, this well-managed and highly popular destination was located in the northern tier of Oakland County, thirty-three miles northwest of Detroit.

An immodestly large sports and entertainment venue it has since its completion been home to the National Basketball Association Detroit Pistons franchise as well as other Detroit sports franchises.

It also hosted the Detroit Shock of the Women's National Basketball Association, the now defunct Detroit Vipers of the International Hockey Association, and football teams including the Detroit Safari and Detroit Fury.

Before the Palace opened, the Detroit Pistons had lacked a suitable home venue. From 1957 to 1978, the team competed in Detroit's Olympia Stadium and Cobo Arena, both considered undersized for NBA purposes.

The balance of teams and stadiums in Metropolitan Detroit accelerated in the mid-1970s with the construction of the Silverdome in Pontiac, on the western border of then Pontiac Township.

Late that decade, other Detroit-based interests began assessing real estate holdings in the vicinity of the immediately successful Silverdome with an eye on building additional venues that could theoretically accommodate other professional athletic franchises.

All considerations were in play. Some even imagined the Detroit Tigers joining the rush on the Auburn Hills area. National Hockey League (NHL) stalwarts, the Detroit Red Wings, made serious overtures, even taking an option on a choice parcel.

In 1978, Pistons owner, Bill Davidson, elected not to share the new Joe Louis Arena with the Detroit Red Wings and instead chose to relocate the team to the Pontiac Silverdome, a venue constructed for football. There it remained for the next decade.

For a short time, it appeared as if the construction on the Detroit River of the new hockey arena bode poorly for the future of sports complexes in Auburn Hills. That gloom would soon give way to euphoria.

First though, a phase of serious disillusionment transpired under the fancy roof of the too-big-for-basketball Silverdome.

While the Silverdome could accommodate large crowds, it offered substandard sight lines for basketball viewing. Of equal annoyance was a controversial "curtain" that hung at one end of the makeshift basketball court arrangement. The humongous banner succeeded at blocking out the larger interior and affecting an enclosed feeling by creating a barrier that cut off visual awareness of the larger cavernous stadium surrounding the finite basketball floor.

Fans had a partial illusion of being in a compact seating configuration. But a larger truth remained self-evident: this was no logical place for basketball, especially the caliber of NBA-level basketball being played by the fast improving Pistons team.

The curtain was arguably tacky. And while it may have blocked out the emptiness of the surrounding interior, it could not sustain the audio dynamics of the game.

However loud and rowdy the fans became, the energy created was lost in the vast canyons of the monstrous stadium. Instead of being contained and magnified, crowd noise wafted into the atmosphere, defusing the amperage of what should have been an emotionally satisfying fan experience.

Everyone knew a replacement facility was badly needed for the hungry young Pistons franchise. But few could have dared imagine the splendor of what would follow. A group led by Davidson built the Palace of Auburn Hills for a relatively modest cost of $70 million, using entirely private funding.

And that is the publicly accepted, fully cleansed version of what was, of course, a much more complex chronology. Certainly, great intrigue accompanied the saga of what professional team ended up playing where and how all the "venue" deals went down.

Needless to say, the City of Auburn Hills was a major winner in the final sorting out of these questions.

By the late 1980s, Isiah Thomas, Vinnie Johnson, James "Buddha" Edwards, John Salley, Bill Laimbeer, and the other unforgettable members (can you say Dennis Rodman?) of the Detroit Pistons were challenging the Boston Celtics, Chicago Bulls, and Los Angeles Lakers, and racking up back-to-back world championships in '89 and '90 in this bold new arena, with larger-than-life heroes like Coach Chuck Daley, Joe Dumars and company leading this march to ecstasy.

Then, for good measure and to ensure the fans remained engaged in a winning tradition, a new-look squad of Pistons again won an NBA crown in 2004. In doing so, they solidified the legend, expanded the glory, and incited feverish excitement in frontier Southeast Michigan.

Longtime Pistons fans achieved nirvana, and the excitement never went completely away.

Sports fan delirium spread into the larger society infecting most living souls within a five hundred-mile circumference, spreading joy into the heavens, and unloosing giddy happiness among all the major tribes of Michigan-styled mankind.

The main story consisted of thousands of smaller stories as a forceful and focused team of lead actors convened under Davidson's driven direction and made the Palace of Auburn Hills happen in an extremely large way.

Pieces fell into place, not by accident but because the key lieutenants in this battle were tested individuals selected for their tenacity, talent, and capacity to emulate the boss, become him, and take his penchant for excellence to its next logical level.

Epitomizing this model at the Palace of Auburn Hills was its president, Tom Wilson, a Davidson protégé of exceptional pedigree.

Still running the rodeo as this book goes to print in 2008, Wilson has become the public face of not only the Palace, but also all the other venues that came to comprise the stable of outdoor theatres and other entertainment facilities existing under the Palace umbrella.

If movie-star good looks were enough to run such a complex and demanding enterprise, Wilson would be home free. So striking is Wilson he at an early time in his life actually auditioned in showbiz before adapting to the role that has placed him on center stage in the local production field.

The success of the Palace of Auburn Hills is all about the drive for excellence embodied in the personality of Bill Davidson and the support role played by Tom Wilson in creating facilities and franchises that would dominate their respective industries for decades to come.

Davidson, Wilson, and their management team cast their fate with retired Pistons player Joe Dumars, choosing him as president of the basketball franchise and spiritual role model for not only the team, but really the entire Palace concept.

What the Palace did to Auburn Hills and what the Detroit Pistons did to the people of this vicinity were coequal occurrences of the supernatural that cannot be adequately expressed in mere hyperbole.

The larger convening of these truly unbelievable happenings solidified the emergence of what has become one of the area's truly dynamic and adaptive communities and forever laid to rest any lingering questions of whether incorporation was the correct strategy in the early 1980s.

Certainly, a palace was born as the Pistons rose on Isiah's shoulders, and championships became a matter of course, and the outside world discovered this handsome new addition to the Oakland County landscape.

The Palace's large seating capacity ranging from 22,000-24,000 (depending on events), and suburban location made it popular for concerts, various and sundry other sporting events, rodeos, and a wide variety of events, numbering approximately 175 events per year.

The Palace of Auburn Hills is currently the largest arena in the NBA. This has helped the Detroit Pistons achieve the highest fan attendance in the league since 2002.

The Palace has been upgraded frequently in its nearly twenty-year history with luxury suites, private clubs, a food court, and new entrances. In the thirty-three years Davidson owned the franchise, its value increased from $8 million to $429 million, according to a *Forbes* magazine study.

Single millions versus multiple millions aside, it doesn't take an adding machine to calculate the impact having the Palace of Auburn Hills as dominant cultural/corporate citizen of a community has had and continues to have upon Auburn Hills.

More than "a palace," an arena, concert setting, or special events venue, the Palace as it's known locally—and now internationally—is really a living, breathing, hyper-extreme source of intense local identity, dynamism, and energy; a facility so busy, vital, ambitious, and ridiculously successful its mere presence helped transform former cow-grazing fields into meadows of mega-proportioned multiplicity exuding accomplishment and promise.

Chrysler Comes to Town

Virtually simultaneous in time of origin, the arrival of a set of dominant interests of the Chrysler Corporation in the land of Auburn Hills equated to monumental legitimization of the new city's importance in regional and national commerce and high-powered business activity.

The Palace of Auburn Hills and the new and dramatic presence of Chrysler all, more or less, happened at once. Such dual undertakings of this magnitude may not occur again in our lifetime, not in a single city, especially a city so relatively new and of such humble rural origin.

Everyone knows these two bigger-than-life entities emerged from within, changing everything, casting large and dominant shadows on the once quiet woodlands around them. Had people not seen it happen, though, many would be hard-pressed to even believe such parallel developments could occur at once, given the truly awesome dimensions of each eventuality.

Groundbreaking for the new Chrysler Technology Center (CTC) occurred in October 1991, and Chrysler World Headquarters opened on the site in 1996. It was designed to bring people together from all areas that are vital to planning—designing, engineering, building, and supplying components for Chrysler vehicles.

By 1992, Chrysler housed about seven thousand workers. Landscape designs took full advantage of the natural qualities of the site in the Oakland Technology Center, north of Featherstone Road, east of I-75, west of Squirrel Road, and south of Galloway Creek.

The four-story megastructure occupies 3.3 million square feet on a 504-acre site, and its construction cost exceeded $1 billion. Then chairman Lee Iacocca said CTC would be the finest automotive technical center in the world.

"Nobody will have the kind of tools we'll have to design and develop products for the next decade and the next century. But it will be just a tool—just bricks and mortar and sophisticated technology. What will really breathe life into CTC is our people. It's designed to help people work together better than ever before—designers, engineers, manufacturing people, procurement people, everybody. This is a monument to the beginning of the end of short-term thinking in this industry and in this country."

At completion, the CTC brought a landmark revelation—twenty-one thousand people worked in the city, more than lived in the community. Most of the jobs had been completed in the last half of the 1980s. Auburn Hills was, by all definition, on the verge of becoming a boomtown.

Its ascendance as a commercial giant was assured when it was designated by state officials in the early 1980s as one of three areas in Michigan to be developed as research and technology centers. The others were Wayne State University and the Ann Arbor area.

Open land in the former Pontiac Township and enviable access to major highways lent the way for such consideration.

Ground was broken by Comerica Bank in the Oakland Technology Center in 1983, the same year Auburn Hills became a city.

Others took note, and the rush was on. Major Detroit developer Schostak Brothers brought in tenants, which soon housed companies like GMF Robotics, Electronic Data Systems (EDS), and ITT North American Automotive.

Automation Alley

In an effort to combine vision and talent to help transform Southeast Michigan into a high-technology powerhouse, the term Automation Alley was coined by governmental officials and embraced by a dynamic organization of leaders from all backgrounds and business sectors.

And again, the City of Auburn Hills was cast as a primary center of this ambitious effort which traces its genesis to Oakland County Executive L. Brooks Patterson's 1997 State of the County address.

In the speech, Patterson unveiled his vision for leveraging the combined strength of the county's high-tech companies into a national marketing strategy that could be used as a tool to attract skilled talent and cutting-edge businesses.

An original member roster of forty-four organizations began the first phase of development, which led to trade missions and the subsequent establishment of an export center designed to assist small—and medium-sized companies become export ready; the center evolved into the Automation Alley International Business Center (IBC).

In October 2001, Automation Alley affiliated with the Great Lakes Interactive Marketing Association (GLIMA) to form an association for technology professionals. This action of joining companies and individuals together created a powerful communication network that had not existed before in the state of Michigan.

Eventually, eight GLIMA Network chapters had formed throughout the state. By April 2004, Automation Alley headquarters was constructed in Troy, south of Big Beaver between John R. and Rochester roads.

Maintaining a strong presence in Auburn Hills, as well as throughout the region, Automation Alley continues to drive the growth and image of Southeastern Michigan's technology economy through a collaborative culture that focuses on workforce and business development initiatives.

In actuality, Automation Alley extends through several counties in Southeast Michigan, winding from Ann Arbor to many points north and east. In the imagination of area residents and business interests, Automation Alley achieves its most vivid definition in the Auburn Hills/Orion Township/Troy corridor where the I-75 interstate freeway sweeps across the heart of Oakland County, vivifying our legacy and our shared futures.

Behold: the Great Lakes Crossing

Ten years after the surge of development creating both the Palace of Auburn Hills and the Chrysler corporate headquarters nearby, another epic occurrence again recast the identity of this reeling-from-redefinition community that continues to wrap around the northeast borders of the City of Pontiac.

Coming in the form of a larger-than-enormous "shopping mall" that in its inception and development defied that common term, the Great Lakes Crossing manifested with such magnificence it seemed to nearly shake the planet, stun the area populace, and alter the frequency with which most consumers felt compelled to exercise their prerogative.

Blending the hottest concepts in theme entertainment and dining with an unparalleled offering of more than two hundred exciting, value-oriented, and regular-priced stores, the gigantic mall opened in November 1998. It boasted six themed and architecturally distinctive areas in a 1.4 million square foot structure. Walkers taking one lap around its inside parameters log eight-tenths of a mile; if they include entrance hallways, make that 1.08 miles!

Great Lakes Crossing brought many firsts for Michigan, including Bass Pro Shops' "Outdoor World" (a five football fields-large store setting featuring outdoor gear, natural motifs, and other attractions); GameWorks, a high-tech playland developed with guidance from Steven Spielberg; the Rainforest Café; and Neiman Marcus Last Call Clearance Center.

This sprawling and captivating facility went from vision to reality over an extended period of time as developers and real estate interests eventually overcame environmental concerns and objections offered up by nearby residential and commercial interests. Layers of intrigue characterized these various proceedings, setting the stage for eventual development that took into account the disposition of some parties and prevailed in the face of others.

Suffice it to say in this context, a mighty tide of commerce came to the region, both with the core mall and in its broad proximity where hundreds of additional retail expressions followed in subsequent years, making this end of the new city one more boisterous and vital cauldron of insipid activity, creative commerce, and attitudinal wonder.

Great Lakes Crossing became a major destination for shoppers from Detroit's tri-county area as well as visitors from throughout the state, northern Ohio, and Canada. As Michigan's only enclosed value regional mall, it capitalized on the presence within an hour's drive of similar bargain-influenced retail citadels offering to the consuming public over 160 manufacturer outlets and traditional retail stores.

Asphalt enveloped the hillsides around its mighty reach, accommodating seven thousand parking spaces spreading out from its full mile of visible frontage from I-75. Mall tenant space totaled a mind-boggling 545,000 square feet, with gross lease-capable area extending to 1,359,000 square feet.

Overnight, Great Lakes Crossing became both a source of awe and pride, intrigue and wonder, a shopper's paradise of such scale you had to see to believe it. Even seeing it failed to reduce most skepticism that "a mall" could achieve such magnitude and magnificence right there alongside the interstate.

The mall's building "shell" was constructed before any retail tenants had signed leasing agreements. By using steel joists, the owner can economically reconfigure retail spaces based on tenant need according to information on the Web site of the Steel Joist Institute. For example, the open area created by the joists allows signs, graphics, and lights to hang from the roof structure.

In addition, steel joists add visual character to different sections of the mall. Some of the unique effects include exposed steel joists and wood beam supports (for a rustic look), custom-designed joist girders with curved bottom chords, and high-pitched roofs.

Auburn Hills: A City is Born

As an architectural accomplishment as well as a commercial gesture, this horizon-dominating retail configuration that rambles alongside I-75 between Baldwin and Joslyn roads took no prisoners whatsoever in its quest to challenge Mother Nature for dominion of the entire environment. Unquestionably, this mall of malls became colossal in its capture of regional shopping destination bragging rights.

Regional retail considerations would never be the same as its arrival on the scene equated to throwing away whatever rule book for where to go shopping may have existed before it arrived, seven thousand parking spots later. The Great Lakes Crossing Mall was more than a mall and larger than most mere mortals could fathom and its impact on area travel, commerce, and enterprise was entirely outside the conventional.

A property of the celebrated firm, Taubman Centers, Inc., Great Lakes Crossing became one more crown jewel in the company's portfolio of United States regional and super regional malls, located in major markets from coast to coast. Already established as the most productive such company in the nation, Taubman Centers, Inc., through its Taubman Asia subsidiary is extending into international markets.

By 2007, the company described its pipeline as one of the most active in its industry. With headquarters in nearby Bloomfield Hills, exciting new properties are sprouting up in affluent communities from Long Island to Las Vegas and points far beyond.

Yet it was right here in Auburn Hills where the Great Lakes Crossing mall, Taubman's greatest contribution to the home territory of his now global firm, took root in the form of a massive edifice of truly earth-changing significance.

Founded by Pontiac native A. Alfred Taubman, the organization's global reach and luminescent international reputation are now implanted in its founder's home territory, the vicinity known as Greater Pontiac, now largely defined by the young upstart City of Auburn Hills.

Truly a son of Pontiac, Taubman's imprint in the Great Lakes Crossing mall development exists at the twenty-five-year anniversary of the incorporation of the City of Auburn Hills as testimony to the impact one man can have on a community.

Equally evident, the legacy of all the superlative stewardship and civic commitment of the settlers and early leaders of once Pontiac Township endures today and into the open-ended future, connecting an era past with times yet to come in a celebration of commitment, effort and, that's right, momentum.

Leonard Hendricks Catapults Greatness

After the vote to incorporate and the advent of the new City of Auburn Hills in the early 1980s, momentum swelled up, progress percolated, and the "new" city began to reveal itself.

To outsiders, the astounding degree of growth that would follow appeared to take place in a vacuum, spontaneously driven by developers and pure market forces.

To insiders, however, it was obvious every small step of change was scrutinized thoroughly and filtered through the microscope of local government, particularly at the new city level.

One individual in particular was hired by the new cast of powers that be in Auburn Hills to ride shotgun on the entire emergence of new enterprise and infrastructure.

His impact on outcome was of great significance, and his compelling personality and quiet dignity are forever imposed on the uniquely cogent and orderly city today's citizens take for granted.

Leonard Hendricks entered the scene on February 20, 1984. As the new city's first appointed city manager, this fifty-nine-year-old figure of George Washington-like significance in the chronicles of a newborn city made a huge difference as Auburn Hills was about to take on entirely post-urban dimensions.

With Hendricks running the show, the City of Auburn Hills was ready for prime time, which was a good thing because prime time was less than a moment from eventuality.

Trained as a civil engineer at what became Lawrence Technological University, the Mississippi native had a richly textured resume focused in city management functions undertaken and accomplished during a career spent mostly in the metropolitan Detroit area.

As its first city manager, Hendricks saw his mission in Auburn Hills as both economic development facilitator and protector of the status quo regarding the community's overall interests.

During his less-than-a-decade tenure, Hendricks became the working equivalent of the "force of nature" design. Gently natured and awash in expertise, he gained the respect of the many hundreds of fortunate souls who were lucky enough to come in contact with him.

The closer their proximity, the greater his colleagues' admiration became of this epochal figure in the growth and sense of dignity surrounding the city.

"This man not only had the talents it would take to be an effective City Manager for the new city, he had the personality and charisma it would take to put this little community on the map," Vicky Valko wrote.

"At first, as with any new boss, there was much apprehension. What was this new leader going to be like? Could he change things for the better? Or would he make them even worse than they were before?"

Soon she and others discovered Hendricks had a way of improving things and imparting a feeling of pride city workers felt in their accomplishments.

"People looked to him for more," his colleague, the future city treasurer, wrote.

"It was truly amazing to sit back and watch the change in people, just because of this new man in charge."

Hendricks was friendly and open. He would stop on the way to work to talk with anyone he encountered. Strangers and common city workers alike picked up on his sincerity and goodness and sought to emulate the new standard he embodied.

Hendricks's sincerity extended into community affairs, and his enthusiasm spread throughout. People from all segments of society came to him for counsel and encouragement, which he doled out with ease derived from a life of purpose and a heart of common goodness.

"He never expected you to do something he would not do himself," Valko wrote. "That's probably why so many people respected him."

When it ceased publication in 1991, the publisher of the former newspaper, the *Auburn Argus,* wrote about the development of the city and cited Hendricks's unique contribution and solid reputation among those with whom he interacted.

"He was hired when Pontiac Township was voted out," wrote Jim Sherman. "He had to oversee maintenance of roads, sewers, lighting, and improving them . . . the regular city business."

Upon his arrival, Hendricks cited the appeal of the area—"a nice residential area with growth going on around it." Sherman found that ironic.

"Look at what Auburn Hills is today," he wrote. "Look at what it has in recreational and industrial development."

Not lost on Sherman—or anyone else for that matter—was the extent to which Hendricks's solid leadership helped shepherd in such massive redefinition of an area.

"Hendricks was up-front, totally involved in all of it," he wrote. "All the ordinances, the zonings, public hearings, legal negotiations . . . being the top man in the fastest growing high-tech area in the nation for seven years . . .

and seeing that the right people were hired to do all the sundry jobs required to carry out city services.

"He's Auburn Hills's main man, and please don't ever forget it. He's also unselfish, compassionate, understanding, warm, and friendly. He shows he likes people."

Hendricks, who served three years with the U.S. Marines in the Pacific during World War II, brought confidence and calm to the swirling minutia set in motion by cascading change in the new city.

His self-effacing manner and absence of pretense defrayed conflict and imparted directional hues taken seriously by his minions within a fledging city government.

As Auburn Hills became Oakland County's fastest growing municipality, Hendricks kept things in perspective by being true to his unique roots and steadfast with courage under fire.

The Chrysler development, in particular, was of such scale many area residents were unnerved.

"I know some people are concerned," he said in 1986. "We all resist change. But the benefits outweigh any difficulties that might be created."

Hendricks's words hover in the afterlife, magnificent in prophetic truth. He dared to imagine what others couldn't see at the time—a future Auburn Hills, awash in vitality, fabulous reputation, diversity, enduring commerce, a sense of mission, and a confident future.

Leonard Hendricks will live forever on the Mount Rushmore of the city he helped grow from infancy to adulthood. While it is unlikely a stone mountain will be recast with his image alongside others, his legacy will endure for it is of such dimension it could never disappear, not in a culture that values such heroic contributions.

Hendricks retired in May 1992 after eight years' service.

"I'm leaving the city in pretty good hands, so I feel pretty good about everything," he said at the time, using the word "pretty" twice in one sentence, revealing his native Southern charm and creating an opportunity for at least one writer to kid a great man about a simple allusion.

Under his direction, the city attracted institutions such as the Palace of Auburn Hills, the Chrysler Technology Center, and Comerica Bank headquarters, among hundreds of other prestigious corporate citizens.

In his days in the city manager's chair, Auburn Hills seized the moment, gave itself an entirely new face, body, soul, and mind, and became a beacon of visionary development.

With Hendricks managing every detail of evolution, this new city in the hills evolved into nothing short of sheer civic wonder, a textbook example of what can happen when planners with exceptional aptitude interact with the entrepreneurial class and prove everything *can* change in a heartbeat.

Hendricks was succeeded by one-time Department of Public Safety Director Dennis McGee, yet another exceptionally competent public official who honored Hendricks's legacy by enforcing similar standards with similar dignity and professionalism.

Looking back on this sequence of events, it is worth noting the significance of the one-time local newspaper bestowing such specific attention on the positive role Hendricks played in setting in motion the sequence of events that would deliver a new city from ambiguity to respectability.

Sherman's reveal of Auburn Hills's first—and now legendary—city manager seems certain to endure for its relevance is without question and its implications for the future remain integral to the way governance is undertaken in the halls of officialdom at 1827 N. Squirrel Road.

In Their Own Words

City Treasurer Vicky Valko assisted in the transcription of Hendricks's recollections of his days as city manager, all sections of which appear verbatim in this text. Also included are remarks from the city's mayors, Jim McDonald, Tom McMillen, and Mari Edwards.

Leonard Hendricks

In 1969-70 the Detroit Water and Sewage Department, in cooperation with the Oakland County Drain Commissioner and the Macomb Public Works Commissioner, built the Macomb-Oakland Sanitary Interceptor. This sanitary interceptor made available sanitary sewer service to the northern part of Pontiac Township. SEMCOG projected the population of Pontiac Township would more than double in a decade with availability of the sanitary interceptor. The projected residential development did not happen because the northern part of Pontiac Township is in the Pontiac School District, not known as a strong district. Pontiac Township had a debt for the sanitary interceptor that had an annual payment of about $600,000 and very little development to help pay the debt.

Pontiac Township officials and later City officials did everything they could to provide funding for the sewer debt, including promoting economic development (slow), a sewer special assessment for vacant land (lost in court), and low-income housing on the Chrysler site (rejected by the federal government) with no success.

In the early 1980s, the business census showed that Pontiac Township had a total of 3,000 persons working in the township, including the staff at Oakland University and Oakland Community College.

Pontiac Township had an adequate staff that provided essential services required by the residents.

Pontiac Township residents worked in the auto plants in Pontiac, did construction work, or were employed as office workers and as salesmen. Most of the residents supported the Township form of government.

When the City of Auburn Hills was formed on December 31, 1983, the City Council priorities were to transition from a Township form of government to a city government format, encourage development, and hire a City Manager. A municipal consultant, Don Oakes, had assisted the officials with the incorporation, writing the City Charter, and recruiting and hiring a City Manager. Don Oakes was originally from Alpena, Michigan, where he had served as City Clerk and City Manager. He also served as City Manager for Berkley and Grand Rapids.

After interviewing and considering several candidates, the City Council in early February 1984 approved hiring Leonard G. Hendricks, as the City of Auburn Hills's first City Manager.

Hendricks, a registered professional engineer, had served 12 years as the City Manager of Sterling Heights and nine years as City Manager of the City of Clawson.

In 1983, Comerica Bank purchased the parcel of land between Squirrel Road and the Clinton River north of Hamlin Road. They constructed their computer center on the banks of the Clinton River.

The Seyburn parcel, between I-75 and Squirrel Road and between University Drive and Featherstone, was acquired in the 1960s by Sam Frankel and Associates.

In the summer of 1984, Comerica Bank purchased the Seyburn parcel. In December 1984, Chrysler Corporation took an option on the south part of the Seyburn parcel for the Chrysler Technology Center. Phil Houdek of Schostak, on behalf of Comerica, planned, platted, and promoted the Oak Tech Park.

When Chrysler took the option on the parcel of land at Featherstone and I-75, they started negotiating with the State of Michigan for infrastructure support for the project. The State agreed to schedule improvements to I-75 and M-59, provide a $14.2 million grant to the City for road improvements, enact legislation to establish a technology park district (which provided tax abatements), and provide inspection services for the project through the Michigan Department of Labor.

When it became known Chrysler had an interest in the project, a number of smaller companies started locating in Auburn Hills. Some of the first developments were along Opdyke Road and Doris Road. Comerica developed West Entrance Drive and attracted EDS for their Computer Center and several other computer related companies.

The City extended a water main in Giddings Road to Brown Road to serve Leaseway on the south side of Brown Road, west of Giddings. This water main extension, plus sanitary sewer extensions, provided for development along Giddings, Harmon Road, and Brown Road.

In late 1984, the City started the process to establish two Tax Increment Finance Authority (TIFA) districts. One district is south of Featherstone (including properties in the Avondale School District) and the other district north of Featherstone (including properties in the Pontiac School District). The City Council decided they would capture 50% of the increased taxable value and pass on to all the taxing units the other 50%. The City Council set a public hearing on the proposed TIFA districts. This resulted in extensive, difficult negotiations. Both the Avondale and Pontiac School Districts objected to the creation of the TIFA districts. With the assistance of Attorney John Donohue, in March 1985, agreement was reached with the two school districts. After the agreements were approved, the City Council approved the two TIFA Districts.

Representatives of the Detroit Pistons approached the City in the fall of 1985 with a proposal to build a basketball arena on Lapeer Road, just north of I-75. The City Council supported the proposed arena, and planning for the project proceeded. As planning progressed, the project grew from 100 suites to 140 suites. The final arena contained 182 suites. The project grew from $45 million to close to $90 million.

In January 1986, after having a financial study by Bob Studt, a financial consultant, the City Council considered a proposal to increase the water and sewer frontage charges and capital charges. The City Council decided to postpone the proposal for 30 days to give public notice. During the thirty-day period, 36 projects were submitted to the City. They were allowed to pay the capital and frontage charges under the old rates for a total of over $3 million. This provided sufficient funds to make annual payments on the interceptor sewer debt. After the 30-day period, the City Council approved the proposal for the increase in the water and sewer capital and frontage charges. These fees provided funding for the sewer debt as well as the expansion of the water and sewer system as needed.

As Supervisor Bob Grusnick had a full-time position, but as Mayor of the new city it became a part-time position. During the period preceding the incorporation of the City, Grusnick arranged to open a party store on the southwest corner of Auburn Road and Adams Road. This business provided for his family and allowed him to be available at various times during the day for meetings concerning City business. Many of the businesspeople involved in the development of the City found having a cup of coffee with Bob in the party store was an easy way to get his ear. These included Bruce Gibson of Comerica and Phil Houdek of Schostak.

The Department Heads for the newly formed City had previously served the Township. They included Veronica New, City Clerk; Dorothy Babb, City Treasurer; Bob Rayner, Police Chief; Larry Flanigan, DPW Superintendent; Larry Murray, Assessor; and Arthur Petersen, Fire Chief. Bob Rayner left in December 1985 to go to Comerica as Director of Security. Dorothy Babb was ill and would come in for a period of time and would be off for a while. In Dorothy Babb's absence her Deputy, Elaine Goebel, would fill in for her.

In the summer of 1984, Joe Kelly, a retired Engineer from the Detroit Water Department, was hired as DPW Director. In March of 1986 Larry Murray resigned as Assessor. Harry Reese, Building Official, resigned in February 1986. Dennis McGee was hired in March of 1986 as Public Safety Director. Elaine Goebel was appointed Treasurer in November 1986. John L. Dalton was appointed as the Deputy Public Safety Director and was eventually promoted to the position of Director of Public Safety. Mark Walterhouse was appointed Fire Chief after Chief Petersen retired due to illness.

Among the key people that served the Township of Pontiac and continued to serve the City of Auburn Hills were attorney William P. Hampton and his associates, Ernie Orchard and his associates as the civil engineers, John Everhardus and his associates as the community's bond counsel, Steve Lehoczky and his associates as the local planning consultant, and H. Ford Prince as consultant for pensions and insurance.

In 1984, the Library was established after approval by the voters. It was housed in the Seyburn mansion. In November 1987, the City accepted the Brunette House for the Library. The house was relocated to the Civic Center Complex and renovated for the Library in 1989. In 1994-1995, the City sold Library bonds and expanded the facility.

Glen Schoonfield was hired in February 1986 as Assistant City Manager for Building Services. In July of 1986, Victor Bennett was hired as the City Assessor and Daniel Agacinski was employed as Finance Officer.

As planning proceeded on the Chrysler Technology Center, regular meetings were held with City staff, Chrysler representatives, Comerica representatives, City consulting engineers, the Oakland County Road Commission, and the Michigan State Highway Commission. These were productive meetings and aided in keeping all the related projects on schedule. Area development authorities assisted the project by making 20-year projections on development of the area and projected the traffic volumes on I-75, M-59, and the major County and City roads. Their staff worked over the Christmas holiday in 1985 to provide these projections.

As financing for the Chrysler Technology Center infrastructure, the City Council and the Local Development Finance Authority (LDFA) Board approved a $38 million bond issue to be repaid from the LDFA revenues. The infrastructure projects included Featherstone Road from Opdyke to Squirrel Road, Squirrel Road from Featherstone to Hamlin Road, and Hamlin Road from Squirrel Road to Adams Road, plus the Chrysler roads around the project.

In 1988, the Michigan Department of Transportation awarded contracts to widen I-75 to four lanes each way through the Auburn Hills area. The contract had a bonus provision for completing the project ahead of schedule. The summer of 1988 was hot and dry, and the contractor made excellent time thus earning a bonus of $1 million.

In the meantime, service businesses including restaurants, hotels, and motels located in Auburn Hills.

During this period of time, the planning and land acquisition was underway for a project that became known as "Great Lakes Crossing." This project was delayed because of financial difficulties of the developer from Washington, D.C. The project was reactivated and completed in 1997-98 with a new partner, Taubman.

In November 1986, the City Council submitted a proposal to the voters to pave all the gravel streets and the proposal passed.

In April 1987, Bruce Potthoff was appointed as DPW Director, and Mary Ann Miller was appointed as Economic Development Coordinator.

In 1989, the City started planning for a new DPW Building. In 1990, work proceeded on the construction at the Brown Road site. The new building was named the "Walter G. Smith DPW Facility."

In the summer of 1991, Chrysler began to occupy the Chrysler Technology Center.

When the bids on the street improvements (Featherstone, Squirrel, Hamlin, and Chrysler Drive) were received, they were substantially below the engineer's estimates. Therefore, all of the $14.2 million MDOT Grant was not needed.

It was proposed to construct a four lane divided road on Squirrel Road between Featherstone and Walton Blvd. MDOT approved transferring part of the grant to the Squirrel Road project. After long and difficult negotiations, the City purchased the needed right-of-way on the east side of Squirrel Road from Oakland University. Construction of the Squirrel Road project took place from 1992 to 1994.

During these early years of the City of Auburn Hills, with Mayor Grusnick's leadership, the City Council encouraged, supported, and voted for measures including rezoning, tax abatements, and tax increment financing for improvements. Their actions resulted in the development of Auburn Hills.

An additional TIFA District was established in 1986. These districts were more successful than anyone ever dreamed. Revenue from the TIFA Districts financed many of the City and school projects including fire stations, a public safety building, community building, and improvements for the Village of Auburn Hills.

With capable city staff in place, Chrysler Technology Center in operation, the Palace of Auburn Hills operating in a very successful manner, development continuing through the City, and the Squirrel Road Project ready to begin construction, City Manager Hendricks advised the Mayor and City Council Members of his retirement date of April 30, 1992.

Jim McDonald

James D. McDonald was elected to the City Council in 1989, served as Mayor of the City from 1994 to 1999, and continues to serve as the senior member of the City Council.

During his tenure, there were many things that occurred in the City that made it a better place to live and work. His primary goal was to give back some of the amenities to the community, sort of a payback, for the progress that occurred as a result of the business coming to Auburn Hills. The TIFAs were created, and the City benefited from the tax increment capture revenues. We made use of the funds through improvements to the sidewalks, the roads, drain improvements, and improvements to the infrastructure in the downtown Village Center.

Auburn Hills is a nice place to live, but you don't have the expenses that other communities have because of the support of the businesses with the TIFAs and the business-related tax base. As a result of that growth caused by the businesses coming to Auburn Hills, the City has been able to pay cash for just about everything. We don't have the long-term outstanding debt here that other communities are experiencing.

During his reign as Mayor, some of the items he is most proud of include the fact that the tax millage rates for the City portion of the taxes were never increased since 1993. In fact, the residents experienced a decrease in the City rates every year from 1995 to 2006.

In 1994, a proposal was brought to the City Council to disband the Police Department and contract the services through the Oakland County Sheriff's Department. After a lengthy review and consideration of the proposal, which included a great deal of public input, it was decided by the City Council to maintain its own Police Department. The community felt there was a great value in having our own department and felt very strongly about keeping the Department. They wanted to keep the community involvement that they had experienced with our own department.

In 1994, the City Council approved an agreement with Wayne Disposal regarding the landfill located at the southwest corner of Lapeer and Brown Road. Under this agreement the City received revenues from each truck carrying a load into the landfill. The revenues resulting from this agreement were used to fund many programs here at the City.

In the early 1990s, the City purchased the Hawk Woods Nature Center located on Bald Mountain Road, from the Pontiac School District. In early 1993, we started the redevelopment of the park in order to provided better amenities to the citizens. On June 10, 1995, the City rededicated the park as the E. Dale Fisk Hawk Woods Nature Center.

In 1996, the City partnered with Chrysler on the City's use of Chrysler vehicles for its fleet of vehicles. Their evaluation of the fleet programs was based on the vehicles used for Police cars. The City has used Chrysler vehicles for many years, and now Mattel has even modeled one of its Matchbox cars after a City of Auburn Hills Police Vehicle.

History was made in Auburn Hills in 1997 when Doreen E. Olko was the first female to be appointed to the position of Police Chief in the City of Auburn Hills. With our new Police Chief, the City adopted a more progressive management style within the Police Department. There was a modification to the chain of command, there was a clearer division of responsibilities, and we enhanced services to the citizens of the community.

Mr. McDonald was also very instrumental in having the City Council meetings televised. By advancing the City Council meetings technologically, more of the citizens can be aware of the decisions being made by the City leaders and also what is happening within their community.

In order to help streamline the City Council meetings so they would not run into the late hours of the evening, and to also allow the Council to be more productive with their time together, Mr. McDonald requested that all land divisions and site plans to be placed on what is known as the Consent Agenda. This allows several routine items to be considered for approval at the same time if there was unanimous vote of approval from the Planning Commission. If anyone present at the meeting would like to discuss the matter, then it is removed and considered in its normal sequence on the agenda.

In November of 1998, the City approved the M-59/Squirrel Road interchange, opening up the passageway to the Village Center, providing better access to Oakland Community College, Oakland University, and all of the new business headquarters which are located in Auburn Hills.

In March of 1999, the City approved the design of the new Public Safety Building which would be constructed at the northwest corner of the Civic Center Complex. This facility, paid for with cash, would eventually become home to our Police and Fire Departments, providing the staff a state-of-the-art facility which would greatly improve the services to the community. The ribbon-cutting ceremony for the new facility took place on July 23, 2001.

The City worked very hard at getting the environmental issues resolved. This included getting a contaminated junkyard, the property formerly known as Taylor Road Auto Parts, cleaned up. This land became part of what is now known as the Fieldstone Golf Course.

In June of 1998, the City Council created the Brownfield Redevelopment Authority. This Board was created to help address and clean up environmental issues within the City. Having the Brownfield designation allowed the City to capture incremental tax revenues on contaminated land and use those revenues to assist in getting the contamination cleaned up. The end result is that the contamination or the source causing the contamination is gone, the land can be developed, and the tax base is increased due to the improvements on the property.

In July of 1998, the City opened Fieldstone Golf Course, which was designed by Arthur Hills. The designer took the former Arrowhead Golf course, which was a 27-hole golf course, and upgraded the course into one of the best 18-hole courses in Oakland County.

In 1999, the City dedicated a section of land at Pontiac Road and Phillips Road as the Dennis Dearing Jr. Memorial Park. This park is named after a member of our Fire Department who lost his life in the line of duty.

The City Council voted to purchase the land formerly owned by Grand Trunk Rail Road for a trailway system within the City. The land was purchased in 1999, and the City continued to make improvements to the trail. When the Michigan Department of Transportation improved I-75, north of Square Lake Road, they widened the freeway, so the City Council in conjunction with the Michigan Department of Transportation installed a $1.5 million pedestrian walkway over I-75, creating another amenity for the citizens. This walkway is connected to the Clinton River Trail and connects the trail from the City's western boundary at Opdyke Road to its eastern boundary at Adams Road.

Tom McMillen

Though I was only Mayor for two years, our growing city continued to grab some of the most prominent businesses in the Midwest. We continued to work hard to make sure we balanced the needs of the business community with the desires of our residents.

I was pleased that we were able to reduce the tax rate while providing high quality services to our residents and businesses.

The services to our "seasoned citizens" and our youth became more popular. More crowds were at our parks, and there were more opportunities for our community members.

I was involved in numerous ribbon-cutting ceremonies for new businesses and helped welcome them to Auburn Hills.

Mari Edwards

During my tenure as mayor I have seen a mix of development activities in the city. Some neighborhoods and commercial developments have matured while others have just begun. The commercial base has remained strong showing continued growth even during a statewide economic slow period. I have been able to be a part of unique methods both locally and in partnership with state and county agencies that have been applied to continue assisting business development.

The strong business base continues to afford services, programs, and facilities for the citizens that are on par or exceed neighboring communities. Most significantly, I have been party to the Village Development and the construction of several beautiful facilities including the Golf Course Clubhouse, the Public Safety Building, City Hall, and the Community Center.

I should not fail to mention that during the recent years the City has turned more and more toward concepts of environmental sustainability. Water quality, construction standards, property stewardship, and the general aesthetic appearance of the City have become an integral part of Auburn Hills. All one has to do is to look at the many parklike roadways; the rivers and streams; the parks, paths, and trails; Fire Stations and Public Services properties; and Civic Center grounds to see the results the City's emphasis on appearance and environment.

As we move into to the 21st century, I am confident the foundation and framework that have been established will allow for even more success in the future of Auburn Hills.

Part 3

A City Comes of Age

A City Comes of Age

The City of Auburn Hills meets the year of 2008 with a lively history, a proud tradition of civic accomplishment, and a most promising future.

Its institutions and governmental structures have matured into ripe, optimally functioning entities providing support and services to an erudite and cosmopolitan citizenry.

Unique harmony has been unleashed within this community, fulfilling the vision of its early residents and leadership cadre.

This exceptional outcome is on full display within the inner workings of city government.

The Office of the City Clerk

The responsibilities of, and services provided by, the Clerk's Office vary widely. The office provides administrative and clerical support to the city council and recently developed and implemented the use of electronic agenda packets. The Clerk's Office prepares the agenda and records and transcribes the minutes for the council and various other boards and commissions of the city.

This office also administers federal, state, and local elections and maintains the records of all registered voters in the city. In addition and among its other duties, the office is responsible for the dissemination and preservation of official city records, Freedom of Information Act responses, and issuance of certain required licenses and permits, including liquor, trash hauler, public recreation hall, and used car lot licenses.

The Clerk's Office has four full-time employees and operates with a $446,000 annual budget.

The Office of the Treasurer

Of the two things certain in life, the responsibility of the collection of taxes is the responsibility of the treasurer. Records indicate that the treasurer has collected taxes for this area since 1873.

Previously located on Opdyke Road in a small office behind the former site of Fire Station No. 2, the Treasurer's Office had a staff of three: the treasurer, the deputy treasurer, and an accounts receivable clerk. In May of 1977, the municipal officers were relocated to the civic center complex located at the northwest corner of University and Squirrel.

In March 1978, an additional accounts receivable clerk was added to the staff to assist with the expanding responsibilities of the receptionist position. The staff has remained that size since that time.

All monies paid to the City of Auburn Hills are received and accounted for through the Treasurer's Office. The office serves as the central location for all revenue collections and is responsible for all deposits and investments. These include revenues directly collected by the Treasurer's Office and revenues collected by other areas and reported to the Treasurer's Office. This includes billing and collection of property taxes with subsequent distribution of those collections to Avondale, Lake Orion, Rochester, and Pontiac Schools; Oakland Intermediate Schools; Oakland County; Oakland Community College; state of Michigan; and, of course, the City of Auburn Hills.

The Treasurer's Office also processes the following payments: payment for water and sewer usage bills, payments for invoices and assessments, payment for miscellaneous accounts receivables, payment for City of Auburn Hills parking tickets, and the purchase of dog licenses. As part of the growth and expansion of the tax base for this community, the city council approved the creation of the TIFA Districts (Tax Increment Finance Authority) and BRA Districts (Brownfield Redevelopment Authority), which allow the capture of certain designated funds for the development and improvement of the community within those districts.

The Treasurer's Office is responsible for the distribution of those funds from the tax revenues to the authorities. Included in those projects have been the improvement of Squirrel Road, University Drive, the downtown redevelopment that occurred at Squirrel and Auburn roads, and the new construction and expansions of the buildings at the civic center complex.

The Recreation Department

In the late 1980s, city leaders recognized a need in the community for organized recreation and senior citizen programs. Officials decided to contract with Avondale School's Community Education Department for the administration of these programs. An office was located in the "Mansion" on the civic center property, which was the former home of Wesson Seyburn, the owner of the original Seyburn Estate which is now the City of Auburn Hills Civic Center Complex.

On September 16, 1989, an open house was held to introduce these two programs to the community. In 1990, the Auburn Hills Library moved from the front portion of the mansion to its new headquarters in the complex. The recreation and senior programs moved in, and the mansion was officially designated as the Auburn Hills Community Center. In 1993, city leaders chose to officially bring these two programs under the umbrella of the City of Auburn Hills administration, and the programs were renamed the Recreation Department and Senior Departments, respectively. These two programs work closely together to provide recreational and social opportunities for people of all ages.

The Recreation Department, with support from the city council and in partnership with each of the city departments, offers a variety of quality yet affordable recreation programs, services, and special events for the community. From summer camps to music in the parks, youth athletics to adult health and wellness, and everything in between, there are benefits for all residents. Citywide special events have become a specialty of the Recreation Department. Held annually, events including the Easter Egg Hunt and Bonnet Contest, the Ice Cream Social, Concerts in the Park, the Bluegrass Festival, Halloween Trail, and the Fall Festival in the Woods are enjoyed by citizens throughout the community.

The Recreation Department has also led the development and re-development of several recreation facilities throughout the city. This began in 1993 with the redevelopment of the E. Dale Fisk Hawk Woods Nature Center, then the development of the Dennis Dearing Jr. Memorial Park (1999), Manitoba Park (2002), River Woods Park (2003), the Clinton River Trail (2003), the Skate Park (2005), and the new community center (2006). These facilities provide a variety of year-round opportunities for all residents of the City of Auburn Hills.

The Department of Senior Services

The Senior Citizen Services Department, along with the Recreation Department, started out as a part of a contracted service agreement with Avondale School district.

The Senior Services Department shared space in the old library (Seyburn Mansion) with the Recreation Department until 1990 when the library moved to its beautiful building, and Seniors and Recreation expanded into the rest of the building.

In 1993, both the Senior Department and the Recreation Department became official departments of the City of Auburn Hills. From that point forward, there has been tremendous growth in programming and services for the seniors and their families in the community.

One of the more familiar services with a senior program is the Meals on Wheels program. The city contracts with OPC (Older Persons Commission) to provide the food for the senior Meals on Wheels program and site programs. Volunteers deliver meals seven days a week to homebound residents in the community. In addition, meals are served daily to seniors who visit the center.

Transportation is another service for seniors. Through the SMART mileage and Municipal Credits, the transportation program supports two lift-equipped buses. Rides are provided daily for medical appointments, grocery shopping, business appointments, and coming to the center for activities. The Senior Transportation program is funded entirely through the SMART dollars and rider donations.

The Senior Department also utilizes CDBG (Community Development Block Grant) funding to provide Chore Services and Minor Home Repair Program. The lawn mowing and snow removal are for seniors and disabled residents. In addition, the Minor Home Repair program provides free home repairs to eligible homeowners and mobile home owners. The Mobile Home Repair Program is unique to most communities, and Auburn Hills is one of a few that provide these free grants for home improvements.

Other service-oriented programs include the Vial of Life Emergency Information Program, the Knox Box Program, Telephone Reassurance Programs, and Information and Referral. Each year a Health Fair and Flu Clinic along with semiannual blood drives are also offered. Recreational and social programs are a big part of the senior program. Cards, crafts, lectures, and special events are always favorites.

Fitness is a growing program, especially with aging population. The Hilton suites provide their pool free of charge for swim programs. Walking programs and strength building are also quite popular.

The Senior Services Department is quite proud in its partnerships in many community events.

With the growth of programs, services, and attendance, the need was becoming increasingly evident that the current community center was not adequate for the needs of the community. City officials determined that a new community center was needed for both the Senior Department and the Recreation Department. In 2005, ground was broken for a new twenty-five-thousand-square-foot community center.

The design of the building is reflective of other buildings in the complex. Features include a banquet room, catering kitchen, administrative offices, two meeting rooms, game lounge, craft/wood shop, studio, and a gym. The building was funded entirely by TIFA (Tax Increment Finance Authority), a business tax to be used for community improvements.

On May 6, 2006, over a thousand people attended the grand opening of the new community center. Much excitement was in the air as the community finally got a community center to match the needs of the people of Auburn Hills.

The Community Development Department

In 1999, retirements of current positions within the Department of Public Services and Building Services left an opportunity to look into the future and the creation of a newly organized Community Development Department. This exciting new municipal entity would incorporate Planning and Zoning, Building Services, Ordinance Enforcement, and Economic Development to create a "one-stop shop" for all development-related services within the city.

The Community Development Department was officially created with the hiring of a new community development director in August 1999 and was originally housed at the DPS facility, at 1500 Brown Road, from August 1999 until December 2001.

In December 2001, the department relocated to its current home on the main civic center campus, at 1827 N. Squirrel Road. The Community Development Department offices are located in a separate building, between the main administration building and the library on the south side of Seyburn Drive.

The department currently consists of ten full-time employees, one part-time employee, and three contract employees. The department is formally divided into four divisions: Building Services, Planning and Zoning Services, Economic Development Services, and Code Enforcement.

Since its creation in 1999, the department has developed a reputation for high-quality work and exceptional customer service to residents and the development community without sacrificing the community's high standards for development. The department enthusiastically pursues its mission of helping the city council make Auburn Hills a great community in which to live, work, and play.

The Finance Department

The Finance Department is responsible for the financial recordkeeping and reporting function of the city, which has a fiscal budget of approximately $60 million for the 2006 calendar year. The department has the responsibility to maintain the city's financial records in accordance with and to be compliant with the city charter, state law, and generally accepted accounting principles.

The department's primary duties include:

- Maintain accounting records for the City's approximate twenty-five funds preparation of monthly and annual financial reports including coordination of annual audit
- Maintain payroll records and generating all payrolls
- Preparation of all accounts payable checks
- Coordination and preparation of annual budget documents
- Administer City's insurance program
- Maintain and administer the City's pension and retirement savings programs.

The Auburn Hills Fire Department

The Auburn Hills Fire Department has changed immensely from the one-station twenty-firefighter department that it started out in 1942 as a volunteer organization. Today the department boasts of three stations and approximately fifty firefighters. The core beliefs of saving life and personal property from fire remain the same, and there have been several changes since that time.

The Pontiac Township supervisor and twenty men organized and became the Auburn Heights Fire Department on December 14, 1942. Their frontline and only apparatus at that time was a well-stocked 1936 (or '37) Chevy truck. At that time, a citizen had to dial FE 4-6860, the phone number that rang at two gentlemen's houses. Then they would run to the hall, set the alarm, and write the address and type of call on the blackboard.

A second truck was purchased on August 15, 1945, and one of the trucks was then kept at a gas station due to a lack of room at the current fire hall. In 1948, the fire department bought a new international truck, and the Chevy was retired.

The sirens that alerted the firemen of a call were tested daily at 6:00 PM. This tradition carries through to today where pager tests are tested daily at the same hour.

The first fire hall was located at 3434 Auburn Road. Eight years after the department's inception on August 4, 1950, Station No. 220 was built and activated. Before delivery of any apparatus when there was a call for the new station, trucks were pulled from Station No. 210 and driven past No. 220. Men were waiting by the side of the street as the truck slowed down and picked them up. Their first apparatus included a thousand-gallon GMC tanker and a five-hundred-gallon GMC pumper. Only two years later on October 1, 1952, Station No. 230 was put in service. A new one-thousand-gallon GMC tanker was housed there.

In January 1947, years before the new stations were built, a dreadful accident occurred. Lee Koyl's residence was near what is now the corner of Joslyn and Vinewood roads. The residents in the north end of the township had limited knowledge of the township government at the time, including the existence of the Auburn Heights Fire Department.

The Pontiac Fire Department was called for the fire. Citing insurance issues that in effect prevented them from responding, the nearby city's fire responders failed to respond. People thought the house was evacuated. But one of the Koyl's sons hid under his bed and succumbed to the smoke and fire and perished in the blaze. The tragedy as it were hastened the construction of Station No. 220 and Station No. 230.

The practice of sounding the sirens for calls ceased in 1965 when home monitors were installed in the homes of the firemen. Now, firemen carry pagers roughly the size of a deck of cards that will alert them to calls. Some of the larger fires that the City of Auburn Hills has responded to include an inferno at the Pontiac Millworks in 1961, a fire at King Brothers Tractor and Lawn Equipment, and a large fire started by lightning at Church's Lumber in 1974.

From the early days of fire halls large enough to hold one vehicle and alerting sirens, the city now has three stations and a number of impressive apparatuses. Its proud fire department now has three ladder trucks; four engines; three ambulances; a special response vehicle; and nine vehicles used by chiefs, inspectors, or as utility vehicles.

The first firemen held full-time occupations as clerks, salesmen, construction workers, and photographers, to name a few. Today, you may find a truck driver, schoolteacher, construction worker, engineer, or a car mechanic responding to calls as a paid-on-call firefighter.

Sixty-one years later, men and women have volunteered their time, labor, and on occasion their pay to serving the City of Auburn Hills. Putting forth their best efforts, they have helped to keep their fellow citizens' lives and properties protected from fire or natural disasters and the preservation of life.

The transition from the early beginnings to today has not been without turmoil.

Despite the best efforts of the entire cadre, it is unfortunate to note three brave firemen have died in the line of duty, either responding to a call or during firefighting operations.

Fire Chief Mark K. Walterhouse said the City of Auburn Hills Fire Department originated with an all-volunteer force in 1942, serving the then Pontiac Township with notable commitment. Its growth since that point of modest beginnings has led now to a present-day staff of fourteen career and forty part-time personnel serving a residential population of twenty thousand and a daytime population of over sixty thousand people.

On an annual basis, the department responds to an average of 2,500 calls for service with an ISO rating of five.

The department is comprised of three divisions: Administrative Services, Fire Prevention, and Operations.

The Administrative Services Division is staffed by the fire chief and an administrative assistant who are responsible for human resources, planning budgeting, and department records.

The Fire Prevention Division is staffed by the fire marshal, three sworn fire inspectors, and one part-time public education officer. The division offers a variety of services consisting of plan review of automatic suppression and detection systems, testing and inspection of systems, final occupancy inspections, and existing building inspections. The Fire Prevention Division is also responsible for determining the cause and origin of all fires. For our residents, we offer free smoke detectors installed in your home as well as free home fire safety surveys.

The Operations Division is staffed by the assistant chief of operations and forty-eight sworn officers and firefighters, thirty-nine of them are state-licensed basic emergency medical technicians. This division is responsible for the delivery of a wide range of emergency services to the community which include fire and emergency medical response, water rescue, high—and low-angle rescue, and hazardous materials response from three strategically located fire stations.

Chief Walterhouse brings passion as well as expertise to his service to the citizens and business community of the City of Auburn Hills. Those traits are manifest in his overview of his department's commitment to the overall quality of life in this robust community.

"The Auburn Hills Fire Department is trained and equipped to serve the diverse community of residents and businesses that have chosen the City of Auburn Hills as their home," he said. "Our primary goal is to deliver the highest quality of service to all of our customers. Our mission statement is our guide for planning, development, and managing change to ensure that we are meeting our customer's expectations."

The Department of Public Services

The City of Auburn Hills Public Services Department (DPS) consists of several divisions: Water and Sewer Services, Fleet Management, Facilities, Roads, and Grounds Maintenance. In addition to these departments, the DPS is responsible for a large number of areas that do not neatly fit under department categories. Some of those are as follows:

- Sidewalks, trails, and paths
- All city-owned building maintenance
- Rivers, open drains, and ditches
- Maintenance of outsourced contracts
- Engineering
- Parks maintenance and operation
- Public gardens
- Right-of-way and public grounds
- Environmental compliance
- Banner maintenance
- Village holiday lighting
- Roadway dead animal removal
- Purchase and maintenance of all city vehicles and equipment
- Street lighting

- Special event support
- Street median maintenance
- Capital construction
- Municipal parking lots
- Cemetery
- Nature center maintenance
- Community emergency response
- Annual spring cleanup
- Landfill liaison

- The DPS maintains the nearly seventy miles of city roads and coordinates activity with the Road Commission and M-DOT, Michigan Department of Transportation, for all other roads. Winter ice and snow removal is a very high priority for plowing of residential streets.

- The DPS also lends support services to a host of other activities and events city wide.

Assessing Department

The Assessor's Office annually discovers, lists, and values a taxable property within the City of Auburn Hills. The authority is derived from the Michigan Constitution, state statutes, and the city charter. The primary responsibility of the assessor is to develop the true cash value (market value) of property so that in proportion to this value, taxpayers may contribute a fair share of support for the community services received.

The assessor prepares and makes all regular and special assessment rolls for the city. Annually, city appraisers review the new construction that has occurred in the city and review existing properties, and place the appropriate assessed value and taxable values on the assessment roll. Likewise, the personal property in possession of local businesses is reviewed, and appropriate assessments are assigned.

City Manager's Office

The city manager is the chief administrative officer for the City of Auburn Hills and is responsible for the day-to-day operations of the city. The city manager is appointed by and serves at the pleasure of the city council. His role is to implement the policies as set forth by the city council. The city manager also attends all city council meetings and reports directly to the city council on all city matters.

Among other duties, the city manager submits the annual budget, assists in planning strategies to achieve city council goals, and to improve the quality of life in the City of Auburn Hills. This official also coordinates operations and ensures the integration of services among city departments as well as helps ensure the dependable delivery of high-quality services while conserving community resources.

Fieldstone Golf Club

Opened in the late 1990s, Fieldstone Golf Club, located at 1984 Taylor Road, is owned and operated by the City of Auburn Hills and rated as a top municipal golf course in the Midwest. Attributes include ease of playability, condition, scenery, practice facility, service, clubhouse, and dining. Without any doubt, those who evaluate golf courses in Southeast Michigan give this course exceptionally high kudos, including *Golf Digest* magazine, which gave it four stars in its "Places to Play" system.

The City of Auburn Hills Police Department

In 1969, the first police department was established when the present-day city was still a township.

The City of Auburn Hills Police Department provides full service policing to the Auburn Hills community. The department is authorized at fifty-seven sworn personnel and a total staff of seventy-three employees.

The department is organized into three divisions.
- Technical Services, which includes Communications, Records, Property and Evidence, Internal Affairs, Quartermaster, and Public Administration
- Operations, which includes all patrol personnel and directed patrol
- Investigations, which includes all investigative operations as well as the school liaison officer, crime prevention officer, court officer, and identity fraud task force officer.

The police department budget in 2006 was $10.8 million. The department is housed at 1899 N. Squirrel Road in the public safety facility that was completed in 2001. The facility houses police, fire administration, and the central fire station.

The police department's patrol force handles all manner of calls for service on a round-the-clock basis. A subunit of patrol is its directed patrol unit, whose mission is to reduce traffic crashes by use of what it calls its "Three *Es*"—engineering, enforcement, and education.

A second subunit is centered in the city's retail district. Its mission is to centralize calls for service from that area in such a way as to reduce the impact of the retail area's high demand for services on the delivery of police services to the rest of the city.

The department has fifteen bike patrol officers who are active throughout the community and in its parks. The communications center is a Public Safety Answering Point (PSAP) that dispatches both police and fire using up-to-date technology including enhanced wireline 911 and Phase 2 wireless 911 call handling.

The city's progressively minded police commanders maintain a conventional radio system of their own and participate in the OakWin 800 MHz interoperable radio system serving all of Oakland County. The department provides school liaison services to schools in Auburn Hills including the Will Rogers Elementary School in the Pontiac School District and Avondale High School.

As part of school services, it teaches DARE for elementary students in the community. Its crime prevention officer is very active organizing special events including an excellent National Night Out event in August, an annual Citizen's Police Academy, participation in Avondale and Pontiac Youth Assistance organizations, providing target-hardening surveys to homes and businesses.

The department maintains membership in the Detroit Metro Identity Fraud Task Force along with many federal agencies and the Troy Police Department. The City of Auburn Hills Police Department is among the very few agencies that take action on this particular group of crimes which indeed impact so many people throughout the metropolitan area.

The City of Auburn Hills Public Library

In 1984, a millage for first city library was approved by voters. The library opened in a former mansion in 1986. In 1990, the library moved to larger quarters on campus.

Today, the Auburn Hills Public Library offers a multitude of services to a very diverse population. It belongs to a network of sixty-seven libraries in Southeast Michigan, with a shared automation system for materials circulation. In 2005, it circulated nearly 218,000 items; over 104,000 patrons entered its doors.

The library contains over sixty-three thousand items including books, magazines, videos and DVDs, music compact discs, books on tape and disc, and language kits.

Its budget in 2006 was about $1.4 million, and its staffing level was twenty-seven employees led by Library Director Hester A. Hull.

By 2007, the library offered sixteen Internet computer terminals for the public, wireless access, and a new fiber optic connection for communications. It also provided a new self-check system for patrons who wish to check out their own materials. It also offers homebound services to patrons who are unable to come to the library.

Programs for youth, adult and teens, abound, and its meeting rooms are used by the entire community.

Much-appreciated patrons contributed the two bronze sculptures that adorn the library's magnificent structure, an amazing and most accommodating building that received many positive reviews including an honor award from the American Institute of Architects in 1996.

About the Writer

David Trout Pomeroy was born in 1945 in Detroit and was raised in Birmingham. He has lived in nearly every region of the country and currently resides in Waterford Township with his wife, Bonita, and their two sons.

He is author of many books and has been a writer in the journalism and automotive training industries for more than thirty years. As a newspaper reporter in the late 1970s with the *Oakland Press*, he covered the Pontiac Township beat, forming relationships with civic leaders that endure into the present.

His first exposure to township politics occurred when public meetings were conducted in a drab room in the back of a fire station, when flies buzzed around plainly exposed lightbulbs as early political figures jawed over mundane matters, when men in attendance at local meetings wore bib overalls or blue jeans, when tough-minded women took it upon themselves to make sure someone crossed the *T*s . . . at least once in a while.

He was there after the Pontiac Silverdome was built on the western border of the former township. Like others of that era, he simply stared at it for several years, never quite sure if it was apparition or actuality.

He sat in—amused and intrigued—when the first exploratory parties of expensively dressed attorneys representing various Detroit-based stadium developers began showing up at township planning sessions.

Taking notes now and forming permanent pictures in his mind, he witnessed true culture clash and realized incredible waves of change were about to pound on the shores of a once tranquil community.

Long aware of this remarkable story and still working for a living at the time of its twenty-five-year anniversary, the writer was summoned to embrace pure immersion in the tale. His charge was to take ownership of all the details and share them with the reading universe.

At the time of its publication, he wishes to thank the sponsors of this project for entrusting him with telling the tale, salute officials from the still-new City of Auburn Hills for their cooperation and positive strokes along the way, and, most importantly, to pay homage to the hundreds of players whose dedicated involvement in this chronology of events did surely deliver to metropolitan Detroit a stunning source of pride and identity—a state-of-the-art city in the suburbs, the quintessential civic-envisioning Auburn Hills.

Your names frequent these pages. Your contributions resonate for all of time.